D0167938

FUNDA**MENTAL**IST

STORIES OF A MENTALLY ILL, OBSESSIVE COMPULSIVE,
LEGALISTIC YOUTH GROUP KID TURNED PASTOR.

JOEY SVENDSEN
WITH MATT JOHNSON

ISBN-13:978-0692808887 (BC Words)
ISBN-10:0692808884

This book is dedicated to:

My wife, my parents, my brother, and my friends
who've stood by me and loved me when it wasn't
convenient for them.

I'd also like to dedicate this book to
Brett Favre, just because.

CONTENT

PREFACE

I just had a conversation with my friend, Matt Carter, about this book. My question was, "Should this book be published?" I've asked myself whether these stories are meant for public reading. See, I'm a people-pleaser. I need others' approval. I worry that some of you may think I'm motivated to write for shock value—like, I'm just going for cheap entertainment. I'm also worried that some may doubt the veracity of these stories altogether. Of course, the more entertaining the book, the higher potential for more sales. It's natural for some to believe I'm stretching the truth for the sake of a better book. But Matt and I agree, if the stories are true—and believe it or not, they are—who cares what people think?

My other concern is more obvious. The stories are embarrassing—humiliating, even. I'm not sure I want people to know the dark, bizarre, depressing, and obsessive thoughts I've struggled with for most of my life. I once spent a year worrying that someone was going to hell, all because I didn't clarify my stance in a random theological discussion. I toiled over whether I had stunted the growth of my penis by mastur-bating too early in life. I feared once that my fiancée—who was madly in love with me—wanted to be with another man because she laughed at his joke. Honestly, it's a lot easier to keep quiet about all of these things. But I'm at a point in my life where I care less and less about the implications of true honesty. If something relates to the human experience, I can't find one compelling reason to withhold it.

The truth is, these stories are a part of what's made me the person I am now. They represent real struggles of depression and irrational thinking—struggles I've had since childhood all the way into young adulthood. If I were to withhold these stories, I'd be motivated by pride, insecurity, and my need for approval. And I cannot allow myself to be a slave to these things anymore. The struggle for approval will always be real, but I refuse to give in. I reckon that this book is a solid step in the right direction.

Reflecting on these stories has brought back a flood of emotions. About people with severe mental disorders, I used to think, those poor guys. I was glad that level of crazy didn't apply to me. But I eventually came to the sobering revelation that I, Joey Svendsen, was one of "those" people. I didn't realize this until writing this book.

I've also had moments of sadness reflecting back on 'younger Joey.' My heart broke for that dude and what he had to carry and endure. What's worse, my past irrational thoughts didn't even represent legitimate concerns. There were times my sadness and pain were needless.

But the primary purpose of this book isn't to evoke sympathy for me. The purpose here is to communicate brutal, yet lighthearted, honesty. Though I reflect on real struggles, I also think they're funny and enter-taining. In this book, you will get complete open access to the thoughts of a mentally ill person. Typically, you hear and read these sorts of stories as scientific examples. Sometimes they're written in third person about someone long gone. My challenge here is to throw everything on the table, holding nothing back. I almost succeed. That's right—almost. There were certain things that I couldn't bring myself to share.

So feel free to laugh and shake your head in disbelief at my expense. This is meant to be entertaining. Even though I'm hoping to get a laugh, I also want to shed light on a subject people tend to shy away from. I want to bring the issue of mental illness to the plane of reality.

Some folks reading this are among those closest to me. Others hear me talk on a podcast each week. To each of you, I am not a fictional character. To most of you, I'm a real person you've gotten to know in some way, shape, or form. I'm delighted that through this book, maybe you'll grasp the fact that many people struggle with mental illness. We all must accept the fact that there are people all around us who struggle with depression and obsessive-compulsive disorder (OCD). The brain is the organ that thinks for us. When it's broken and malfunctioning, it doesn't think right.

For those readers also struggling with mental illness, I hope that as you read you can say, "Heck yeah, I'm not alone." I hope this can bring some healing to your heart. There are millions of other people out there just like you. It's easy to assume that no one struggles like you do. But it's not true.

If you do struggle with mental illness, I hope you'll feel freer to open up to others about your experience. Those of us who struggle with mental illness can sometimes get frustrated and angry. Sometimes it seems like people are calloused and belittling toward what they don't understand. But we forget that when we aren't open about our experience, we can share blame in how we are treated by others who don't understand.

The fact is, it's embarrassing to open up about mental illness. But staying silent brings an unnecessary label of shame on ourselves. If we stay silent, we can't bring anyone closer to a deeper level of understanding. And if others don't understand, they can't learn empathy or genuine concern for people who struggle.

Speaking of understanding, some may object to the language and content in this book. Some may think I'm being brash. But, these are true, real-life stories. If this book had a movie rating, it'd be "R." Children, go ask your parents if you can continue. Parents, go grab a Dr. Seuss book—are you out of your minds right now?

These stories were hard for me to write. Some folks may even disapprove of my level of openness, especially with regards to the stories related to sexuality. However, authenticity and transparency were my primary goals in writing this book. I've learned in my 39 years that very little harm comes as a result of being honest about personal human struggles. When people read about the confession, pain, and suffering of others, it builds community. To hear honest stories helps us feel less alone and less self-conscious. Then, the cycle starts all over again—and this is a daggum great cycle to repeat. I tell my story to you, then you tell yours to someone else.

But those with sensitive eyes have been warned. For those of you who will now avoid reading this book, I'd recommend you stay clear from the Bible as well—*"There she lusted after her lovers, whose genitals were like those of donkeys and whose emission was like that of horses," (Ezekiel 23:20).*

Lastly, I believe in God. I believe He's had His hand in walking me through my struggles with mental illness. These are personal stories, not instructions on how to "get better." I make no apologies for that.

But I absolutely have maintained a dependency on God, even though often times I wasn't sure He was helping. In fact, if I had ever been fully convinced God wasn't there, I may have killed myself. God met me in a fully tangible way, and proved my doubts wrong again and again. I know now that He loves me no matter what. There were times when God was silent. Yet He kept gently guiding me toward truth, despite my persistent resistance. Whether you believe in God or not, He's a part of my reality, and my stories are incomplete without including God.

Now it's time to sip your coffee, guzzle some beer, nibble some snacks, and proceed. You will hear things I've never articulated to anyone in this way. I haven't purposely kept anything from my wife. But in writing this book, she's learned things from my past for the first time. So I'll close by saying sorry and thank you for reading. You will probably never see me in the same light again.

Chapter One
THE SINNER'S PRAYER
—

I still remember the intoxication of childhood play on warm spring days. Life was good. After getting our fill of Cap'n Crunch and Saturday morning cartoons, all of the neighborhood kids would meet up outside and play all day long. We had our shared toy infatuations. I had all the normal characteristics of boyhood, obsessed with Skeletor, Luke Skywalker, and Optimus Prime. But what set me apart from those other neighbor kids went beyond your standard toy fetish. You see, I was obsessed with Jesus.

Life Was Church, Church Was Life

My parents were brought up as traditional Catholics and became born-again Christians when I was just a kid. That's when they laid down the junior varsity Christianity for the real thing—you know, where you get serious about Jesus and make him the center of everything.

My parents did a great job raising us to value faith in Jesus. Mom or Dad would lead us in weekly family devotions where we'd learn a spiritual lesson, pray together, and talk openly about God. We were the type of family that went to church on Sunday mornings, Sunday nights, and

Wednesday nights, and I loved every single minute of it. I loved my church, the music, and all the people.

I'll never forget one of the purest moments of childhood faith. I had experienced quite a difficult day. You know, kid problems—tragic stuff like missing Dukes of Hazard because the cable was out, breaking a favorite toy, and being forced to go to school every day. I remember quite clearly when the thought popped in my head that one day we'd be in heaven forever with no more worries or cares of this world. Dukes of Hazard would play 24-7. The cable would never go out, toys would never break, and it would always be summer vacation. I was consumed with Jesus—a little guy full of the joy of the Lord. But remember, our family was born-again. That meant that in order to be OK with God and maintain the joy of the Lord, I had to be a good boy.

I was so good that I even punked out my mom in favor of the Virgin Mary. I clearly remember my dad asking me once, "Isn't your mom the prettiest woman in the whole world?" "Yes, sir," I said. "Well, after the Virgin Mary, of course." If I was going to be good with God, I was convinced that I had to have all of my spiritual bases covered, even if it meant that Mom was a runner-up to Mary in beauty. Despite all that, Mom was my spiritual cheerleader, helping me form a habit of daily prayer and Bible reading by adding "read and pray" to my chore list. This may have been the beginning of my check-list-keeping career.

Getting the Sinner's Prayer Wrong

I've always kept lists. For some, lists ensure sanity. They track progress on a work project. They make sure that you've packed everything for an upcoming trip. I used to carry around lists as early as the fourth grade to remind me to read my Bible and pray. To the average Sunday school teacher, this kind of list could nominate you for Christian of the Year. And if there was anyone worthy of earning salvation, it was me. I've probably said the Sinner's Prayer, like, 10,821 times.

Here's how it would go: Sitting in my bedroom, I would ask God for forgiveness, tell Him I wanted to be saved, ask Him to save me, declare Him as Lord, thank Him, ask Him to be my God from now on—in that order and said correctly. I mean, God is perfect, right? Surely, He's a stickler for getting our checklists right.

Each time I said the prayer, I was unsure if I'd covered all of my bases. Did I leave anything out? I'd pray again to make sure I got the checklist just right. But then I'd realize I wasn't even thinking about God while I prayed. I just recited ritualistic words. If my heart wasn't in it, there was no way God was going to hear me. I'd picture God on His big, white, puffy cloud-throne with His flowing beard. "OK," I'd say to myself, "that time God was definitely in my thoughts." But after multiple times of trying to say the magic prayer, I'd be in tears. Maybe salvation wasn't for me. "Hmm, I don't know, Joey," God would say in a thunderous voice, "I'm not so convinced you meant that. Do it again. But this time, say it with conviction, son." I'd walk out of my bedroom and down the hall. My parents would ask me what was wrong, and I would burst into tears. "I just can't do it," I sobbed. "I can't get saved!"

The Glimmer of Hope That Never Quite Stuck

But there was one glimmer of hope. One day during my devotional time, I ran into Romans 4:4-8.

> *Now to the one who works, his wages are not counted as a gift but as his due. And to the one who does not work but believes in him who justifies the ungodly, his faith is counted as righteousness,*

*just as David also speaks of the blessing of the one to whom
God counts righteousness apart from works:*

*"Blessed are those whose lawless deeds are forgiven, and whose sins
are covered; blessed is the man against whom the Lord will not
count his sin."*

I read the passage, and then I read it again. And again. I asked
myself, "Was this a mistake? Was I reading it wrong? Did someone at
the Bible publishing plant mess up? Salvation is completely free?" I left
my Clemson Tiger-themed room that was covered in trophy shelves,
and proceeded down the hall into the living room, Bible in hand.
"Mom! Dad!" I said in amazement. "I just read something crazy."
I was convinced they'd be equally shocked with my discovery. I read
the Romans 4 passage aloud and asked, "Is this true?" My dad
simply responded,

"Yes, it is." This was mind-blowing. Unfortunately, the joy of that
moment didn't last, and it wasn't until years later that I discovered
this truth again, like it was the first time.

The Fourteen-Point Sinner's Prayer Checklist

Two years passed, and I was still pretty much in the same predicament.
I would go through a round of ritualistic salvation prayers and do my
best to believe it worked, but my assurance would only last a few days.
Then, doubt would creep in, and I had to start all over again.

There was a lot of ground to cover in that prayer. I needed sincerity
of heart, and I had to say all the words accurately. Eternity was
a long daggum time, and if I couldn't get that prayer figured out
and settle the score, I deserved literal hell for my apathy. I was

in deep trouble.

I knew prayer was supposed to be simple. Each time I prayed, I thought it would be different. And yet, it never was. There was always something I left out, and I couldn't be sure that I was really saved. Sometimes I'd say the prayer 30 times in one sitting, trying to get it right. Sometimes I'd have confidence that one of those prayers finally stuck and I'd walk away feeling lifted. Sometimes I'd say it once and my heart rate would slow down. Other times I couldn't get it right and would leave for school in a cold sweat, in tears.

For the curious, here's my comprehensive 14-point checklist on how I was supposed to say the Sinner's Prayer just right:

1. I was supposed to ask Jesus, not God, to save me.
2. I was supposed to ask God, not Jesus, to save me.
3. I couldn't be half asleep when I asked.
4. I needed to get the words right. But if I was too formal about it, God wouldn't hear my prayer.
5. I needed to be sorry enough for my sin.
6. If I was sorry for my sin but didn't think about its gravity when I prayed, God wouldn't hear my prayer.
7. I couldn't forget to declare him as Lord.
8. I needed to be thankful for what Jesus did to be sincere.
9. I needed to be sure that I really did pray the prayer. How could I be sure that I really did?
10. I needed to enunciate all the words right.
11. My mind couldn't be distracted on other things.
12. I needed to say the prayer out loud. Saying them in my head didn't count.
13. I need to have faith when praying. Without faith, there was no way I was saved.
14. I had to ask for heaven. How was he supposed

to know that that's what I wanted if I didn't?

And it gets worse. Because of No. 9, I had to start writing down my prayers so that I would have something concrete to remind me. I'd write down "you asked for salvation" on a slip of paper and tuck it away safely for future review. That way, I could prove to myself later that I had prayed. Every time I had to refer to the prayer file, I'd put a check mark next to it. But then I'd realize that I hadn't written down the date, so I'd throw the slip away, say the prayer again, write it down on a new slip, this time with the date. Later, I would realize that I hadn't written down the exact time, only the date. I'd throw away the paper and begin the process all over again.

My Secret Damnation-Proof File

When I was in college, I hid the salvation file away so that no one would see it. But I needed that paper to exist in order for my salvation to exist. I remember playing video games with my buddies, and in the middle of a joystick thumb cramp, out of the blue, the doubt would creep up on me. I'd have to put the game controller down, retrieve the paper from its secret hiding spot, go to the bathroom, and look at it to ensure I was saved. And yet, even then, I was never sure because the checklist would start swirling around my head again.

Once I'd come to my senses and realize that it didn't matter whether I'd prayed to Jesus or to God for salvation, I'd start believing again that I was asleep when I prayed. I'd convince myself of one checklist item, but doubt my sincerity with the next thought. I'd talk myself into my sincerity and in the next thought doubt whether or not I was asleep again. I figured that God didn't count dream prayers.

In my senior year of high school, I read a case study in Psychology

101 about someone who lost an important sticky note. From the moment it disappeared, he began obsessing, believing there were missing sticky notes everywhere. At bedtime, he'd tear the bedding apart for hidden sticky notes. Eventually the guy started unwrapping the paper off his cigarettes before smoking them. He had to make sure he wasn't going to burn an important sticky note that had somehow gotten lost at the tobacco production plant and wound up on a cigarette-wrapping machine. I've always reflected on how extreme that dude's case was. Man, it must have sucked for that guy. Well, at least I had my salvation checklist.

Chapter Two
THE LIFE VERSE

—

During a month-long sabbatical that my church offers its pastors in their seventh year of service, I met with a psychologist for some counseling that my church graciously foot the bill for.

Near the beginning of the session, the counselor asked me to reflect upon current and past struggles. Responding was easy since many of these struggles were fresh in my mind due to the recent work I'd been doing for this book. I recounted some of the mental processes that were commonplace during my teenage years, and as I reflected on the culprits that likely formed a foundation for my current struggles, I could tell that my counselor's look of shock and empathy was obvious and sincere.

Over the next two hours, my counselor gave me insights on why my problems ran so deep. And honestly, I was taken aback. At first, I thought I'd lay on a couch and talk for two hours about my feelings. Then he'd give me a couple of things to think about and a couple of proverbial pats on the back, leaving me wishing I had spent the last two hours doing something more productive.

To my surprise, this guy was studied, smart, professionally trained, and extremely helpful. He brought to my attention the many ways I was being affected today by my tendency over the years to internalize and even own responsibility for other people's struggles. This is just one helpful nugget that represents his many surprising observations. After I gave him a snapshot of a typical day in my teenage years, I was surprised to see that he was outwardly alarmed, which made clear to me that what I was sharing was not insignificant stuff.

Knowing What to Do But Not Doing It

Now I'll share the snapshot I gave him with you.

It's a spring morning in Charleston, South Carolina. The windows are open, and it's humid. There's a sweet smell of fresh blooms wafting through the window. Fortunately, it's not hot out yet. It's spring, and the windows are open because the weather is still mild enough to cool off the house. I have plenty of time to get ready for school. The sun is shining. Everything's perfect. Then my "life verse" pops into my head, and the serene moment is obliterated.

"Therefore to him that knoweth to do good, and doeth it not, to him it is sin," (James 4:17). This was my "life verse" as a teenager. For those of you who aren't up on Christianese, the "life verse" is the one Bible passage mantra that functions as a spiritual pick-me-up. It is supposed to remind you of God's love and motivate you to live a better life. I chose it because I was constantly aware of my shortcomings, lack of effort to help others, and failure to share my faith with others. For me, it was the one mantra I used as a pump-me-up to love and trust Jesus more. Because I believed I was sinning by what I wasn't doing (sin of omission), my salvation was at stake—not only that, the salvation of others, too. That's why I had to make sure I was all prayed up in the morning— essentially, wash my hands of someone else's blood and their inevitable doom in eternal hell. I had to have all the bases covered, just in case.

Pop Tarts and Prayer

It's only 7:00 a.m. and already my chest feels tight. Along with the tightness comes painful butterflies in my stomach. The angst travels up to my head and throws my mind into a doomed war. There I am, psychic artillery blowing up in my head, and all I have are a couple of cap guns. Before bedtime the night before I realized once again I have no peace about my salvation. I recite the Sinner's Prayer sincerely, but something is amiss. I'm too wordy in my prayer again. It's a dud. I go through the checklist again. As soon as I throw off my covers and my feet hit the floor, I reach up into my closet to retrieve my official record-keeping of the Sinner's Prayer. I have to make sure my mind isn't fabricating an imaginary salvation prayer. Most mornings, I'm not convinced. I have to make sure to get it right.

Once my salvation was secure and my heart rate slowed, I'd take a seat in our hand-me-down loveseat to pray and read Scripture. After all, it was the right thing to do. I'd been told my whole life how important Scripture reading and prayer was. At church, I learned it was the only thing that could keep me living right. If I failed this daily routine, I was doomed to fail in life. Morning quiet time safeguarded against bad things happening. If something random happened later in the day, I could rest assured they were related to skipping devotional time. I'd end up embarrassing myself by randomly puking in class, or I'd trip in front of a pretty girl. Worst-case scenario, I'd send someone to hell out of failure to witness to them.

Skipping daily devotions was an affront to God; it conveyed that I didn't care about living for Him. The last thing I needed was extra guilt. A couple of minutes into my daily routine, my mom would poke her head into the room, give me a motherly smile, and say that breakfast was ready. To my parents, my spiritual discipline was something to cherish. Their young man was growing up to be someone who put God first at the beginning of each day. My priorities were straight.

At the end of the prayer time, though, at least I knew I'd kept my end of the bargain. It was a small victory when I could start my day right by nailing quiet time. That was a win in itself. The next challenge: getting dressed. If I chose the wrong T-shirt, eternities were at stake.

Witness Wear

Things were often easier with the life verse in mind. Take dressing myself in the morning as an example. The life verse took the guesswork out of color coordination and matching styles. If I was going to do right by what I wore, the choice was simple: I had to wear Witness Wear— you know a Christian-themed T-shirt.

When the life verse compelled me to be a witness for Christ, it was clear that Christian T-shirt day was upon me. I had a collection of my own, and my dad had a selection in his closet as well. His shirts were a bit more blatant in the gospel message. Days calling for bold witness meant I'd have to go with the old man's attire.

One of dad's shirts displayed a black crucifixion scene on the front. The back read, "He was wounded for our transgressions." Another shirt had a close-up of Jesus holding out his nail-scarred hand and asking, "Who do you say that I am?" Mine were a bit tamer—for example, a psychedelic depiction of a galaxy with the words, "In the beginning, God." I was compelled to wear these shirts because I was surrounded by lost people who needed saving. They needed Jesus. The T-shirts were brilliant. Wearing my witness spared me the guilt of having sinners' blood on my hands. Jocks, potheads, pretty girls, ugly girls (who are beautiful in God's sight, of course), smart dudes, smart girls, class clowns, the friendly and the assholes—they were all going to hell no matter how nice they were. I was God's messenger, chosen for my high school, and if spreading the message meant meeting wardrobe requirements, so be it.

Inevitably, there was always someone who'd mock my shirt. Every time I walked into science class with my "In the beginning, God" shirt, there was a girl in the front row who would say in her most epic Morgan Freeman-like voice, "In the beginning!" That was her way of calling me a religious weirdo. I had a love-hate relationship with Witness Wear. I didn't like the attention I brought to myself, but knowing I'd been obedient to God in what I wore was calming. Nothing like being snuggled up in the touch and feel of cotton. The touch and feel of God's-Judgment-Reminder Cotton that is. After I'd gotten ready for school, I was ready to go and went through the checklist.

- Salvation acquired to the best of my ability? Check.
- Read Scripture? Check.
- Prayed? Check.
- Christian T-shirt on? Check.
- Received God's favor? Check.
- Stomach full of blueberry-frosted Pop Tarts or toaster strudel? Check.

Car Stereo Witness

It was go time. After starting the car, I'd wait for my next-door neighbor to hop into the passenger seat. We were childhood friends, and he was lost as lost could be. No, he didn't get lost on the twenty-yard walk to my car. He was spiritually lost, man. You know. Lost people stick out like a sore thumb. They listen to secular music, watch R-rated movies, and laugh at jokes. Those people. He was going to ~~hell in a handbasket~~ lost. I think he may have even worn a secular band T-shirt. Oh, yeah. Satan had him. I had to try something. I had just the right thing: Christian rock.

I figured it was a good idea to get some kick-ass Christian music cued up so he'd hear some abrasive gospel-centered lyrics. And when I say "kick-ass," I mean it. To many, Christian music is Michael W. Smith or Amy Grant—syrupy sweet, soft-rock equivalent to pastel-colored floral wallpaper. But fortunately, I'd stumbled upon Tooth and Nail Records, a label that signed legitimate bands—bands that weren't embarrassing to play on your car ride to school. In fact, my neighbor buddy was so impressed with my taste in music, he often wanted to know who we were listening to. Whenever I put a Christian CD into the player, I always imagined my buddy breaking into tears, convinced of his sin and his need to repent. Once he'd start crying, I'd pull over and put the car in park. I'd put my hand on his shoulder and say, "Hey, buddy, it's OK. We're all sinners. We all need Jesus. Why don't you accept Him into your heart right now?" Then, I'd lead him in the Sinner's Prayer right there on the side of the road. The tear-drenched Sinner's Prayer never happened, but at least he was hearing the gospel message through the jams I was pumping. That meant I could wash his blood from my hands when he'd die of a massive head trauma from falling off his skateboard or something. Maybe he'd go to hell when he died. But at least I'd done my part.

Traffic Sign Sins

The problems kept coming, though. Halfway to school, there was a ridiculous traffic sign I couldn't not obey. The speed limit on the sign was 20 miles per hour on a very gradual curve. For starters, I always made quite sure to drive the speed limit. Romans 13 commands us to obey the laws of the land, after all. I certainly didn't want to purposely sin and be a bad example to the younger guys I took to school with me. If they saw me speeding, it'd be a bad influence, and they'd get all kinds of ideas in their head—like having sex with girls or something. I couldn't be responsible for that.

The speed limit was 35 miles per hour, but you could honestly take it up to 45 and still get around the curve, but the daggum sign said to slow down to 20. It was the most bizarre speed limit ever. There was no need for it. And yet, every day on the way to school from 1994 to 1995, I slowed down to 20 miles per hour. I'm telling you, it was ridiculous, awkward, and pointless every single time. But I had no choice. I had to be obedient.

But there were some mornings when it was just too much to bear. I'd resist God and the laws of the land and take that curve at 40 as I prayed for God to forgive me. As I sped like a demon through that curve, I was always haunted by this vague feeling that I'd get into a head-on collision seconds later, and I'd be sent straight to hell with the unrepentant sin of "speeding in traffic" in my heart. Fortunately, there were never any head-on collisions and no deaths.

Now it was time for class. From the time I was in homeroom with the ring of the last bell, I had a job with eternal significance. I had to maintain an adequate Christian witness at all times. I had my Christian-themed T-shirt on, and I spoke about my faith often enough that people knew I belonged to Jesus. But it was up to me to show off my righteousness so that others would want to be friends with Jesus, too.

Cafeteria Witness Fail

The burden continued during lunchtime. I couldn't even eat my dang chicken tenders, French fries and applesauce in peace without having to do another set of spiritual bench presses. There was Jesus spotting me to bench a weight way more than I could lift. "One more! You can do it!" But I couldn't, and I knew it.

Walking into the cafeteria, I was immediately met with the guilt of not sitting by a nerd, a special needs kid, or an ugly girl. Thinking back, there were a few times I sat with kids like that through my high school career, but it always felt forced. Instead, I opted to sit with guys I'd been friends with since middle school. We had the common ground of basketball and cutting jokes. But I took the road less traveled. I didn't crack a smile at perverted jokes and wouldn't admit girls were a turn-on. One time there was a girl wearing spandex bending down next to our table. My buddies kept telling me to look at her, but I just wouldn't do it. I could have at least told them, "Dude, yes, her body parts are hot as hell, but I'm trying to be respectful," but I cowardly ignored them with no explanation. Of course, from their vantage point, my non-engagement meant I was gay.

My friends were perverts, and they were going to hell for it. It was my job to evangelize them. But I didn't have the guts to do it. This is where the "life verse" from James 4:17 came to harass me. "So whoever knows the right thing to do and fails to do it, for him it is sin." Every single day the bell rang after lunch, it was my cue to say a prayer of repentance. I knew I should have witnessed during lunchtime, but I didn't. Every day was the same—until that infamous day my junior year.

A Girl Named Heidel

I met Heidel in 1991 in freshman German class. She was emo before emo was cool. She had long hair, wore hippie clothes, and had great taste in music. She listened to Bad Brains and Jane's Addiction, and everybody with any sort of common sense liked Nirvana, as Nevermind was just hitting the radio waves and cassette players. Not my cassette player, though. Secular music, man—I could respect it. But own it? Nope. Listening to Nirvana would be sinful. What is "Nirvana" anyway? Isn't it like being in a satanic trance or something? Yeah, you bet listeners of grunge were going to burn like Pres-to-Logs in hell for that one.

Though Heidel's music choices were cool/sinful, Heidel and I were buddies. We had fun together, but there was no romantic attraction as far as I could tell. We had a running joke to see who could wear the most ridiculous socks. One Christmas, I got a pair of white socks with black diamonds on them, and I didn't like them much. I gave them to Heidel. She loved them and wore them proudly.

Fast-forward to May 1994. It was just a normal day at school. As soon as I arrived, a friend walked up to me and said, "Did you hear? Heidel killed herself!" I didn't believe it at first. But other kids were talking about it. I saw a teacher in the hallway crying. When I saw the guidance counselor making the rounds, I knew it was real. It was so weird, so sad, and shocking.

Heidel and I didn't hang out after school. We didn't talk on the phone. I didn't know her family. We just got to know each other in German class. That was the extent of it. But I cried that day. Maybe I cried to get attention, I don't know. But once I composed myself, I realized this was no time for crying. I knew what I needed to do. I'd been a coward in the lunchroom all year long. Now was the time to be bold. I had to witness to my classmates. It was my duty to warn them that people commit suicide when they don't find joy in Jesus—and when you listen to bands like Nirvana. I told them, "You'd better find your hope in Jesus if you don't want to end in ruins like Heidel." I shared this message in every class I was in. At least I'd done my part and could rest easy that I'd done the Christian thing to warn my classmates to save themselves from hell. In response, my German teacher said, "You know, Joey, not everyone believes that people who commit suicide go to hell, OK?" Whatever, teacher. I did what I had to do and was free of responsibility. I could wash my hands of everyone else's blood.

Chapter Three
YOUTH GROUP

———

In case you hadn't heard, you can catch sin like you catch a cold. It's best to stay away from the infected. That's why youth group was the perfect place for kids to go to have some good, clean, safe, virus-free fun. In addition to good clean fun, every so often a decent youth pastor would come along, teach the kids some Bible, and inspire them to live godly lives. As it turns out, there's no better place to nurture OCD, depression, and religious legalism than a youth group. Unfortunately, youth group helped to solidify the guilt-ridden, checklist Christianity that was crushing me. Well, maybe, getting "crushed" isn't the right way to put it. Maybe God was just giving me a big hug, and I didn't know it.

Avoiding the Bad Kids

In high school, my friendship rule of thumb was to avoid hanging out with school friends outside of school, because it was too risky. I felt too uncomfortable around vulgar joking. I couldn't stand to be around people cussing; or drinking—man, that was the worst. Well, at least I could hang at the youth group and none of that stuff would be happening.

It's funny though, some of my closest friends in youth group sinned just like the kids at school. They were true friends, they respected me, and they wouldn't dream of sinning in my presence. You see, I was on higher ground and had a better shot at heaven than they did. But every so often, I'd let my guard down around the sin virus. I just had to wash my hands a lot and make sure I was up on my vitamin C intake. I was the guy all the parents trusted. If their kids were out on a Friday night with me, things would get goofy—in a sanitized kind of way, of course—but at least the fun times wouldn't turn sinful. And if things did turn sinful, at least the Sani-Wipes and vitamins kept me safe from catching the sin bug.

I'd acquired a level of respect. I was nice to the popular kids, outcasts, nerds, and geeks. As for my own social standing, I was somewhere in the middle. I had a good sense of humor, people could tell that I was my own person, and I didn't walk the wide road leading to eternal destruction. At least I wasn't dismissed as socially pathetic. I mean, c'mon, I listened to Tooth and Nail bands. That had to count for something! At the end of the school year, one guy wrote in my yearbook, "I hope one day, I'll be brave enough to be myself like you." Speaking of yearbooks, check out my simple, to-the-point yearbook quote:

> *"Do not love the world or anything in the world. If anyone loves the world, love for the Father is not in them. For everything in the world—the lust of the flesh, the lust of the eyes, and the pride of life—comes not from the Father but from the world. The world and its desires pass away, but whoever does the will of God lives forever," (1 John 2).*

Yup. That's me, Mr. Popular.

Um, You Guys Might Go to Hell

In my social holiness club (i.e., church youth group), if you were living in conscious, habitual sin, there's no way you could be in good standing with God. And if you weren't in good standing with God, you could never live a fruit-bearing, productive, on-fire Christian life. How's that for some church lingo?

I discerned that there were some lukewarm kids in the youth group. I'd seen some secular band T-shirts floating around and kids smoking behind the school. Things were definitely not on the up and up, and it was important to take a stand. So one Wednesday night, I told my youth pastor I'd like to share something with the youth group. He gave me the floor, because 17-year-old boys have great discernment when the Spirit is moving. Here's what I said: "I think there are lots of people in this circle right now who would be unsure where they would go if they were to die right now." Mic drop. Yeah, I said it. Translation? Many people are living a lifestyle that prevents them from having the assurance of salvation.

The youth leader seemed irritated and immediately responded, "OK. OK. Well, let's test this." Hoping that I would be proven wrong, he asked, "Who here feels unsure about where they'd go if they were to die right now?" Sure enough, half the hands went up, and the tears started to fall. I emerged as the hero, my youth pastor the zero. I had spoken up and taken a stand. I'd gone against the grain and probably saved many souls from hell that day—until two weeks later when the fear wore off, and all the same kids gradually worked their way back up the sin totem pole.

Something was off. This youth group was supposed to be legit and on fire for Jesus. Many of these kids abided by a contract to be a part of the drama or ministry team. The contract permitted them to only watch

33

Christian-themed or G- and PG-rated movies. And of course, they had to maintain a reasonable curfew. Sinners like to hide in the dark after all. And yet, they all seemed guilt-ridden about their sin. They had no assurance of salvation. Maybe they hid their jacked up-ness more than the others. What I found out was that many of these kids were lying about their obedience to the contract and many were —gasp!—having sex with one another! So-and-so was having sex with her boyfriend. Such-and-such were "doing it" on the church retreat. I was floored. I felt let down because many on the big-sinner list were people I looked up to.

How to Earn Grace through Guilt

Kids in the youth group were blowing it big time. But at least there was a guilt code we could all follow to attain personal holiness. And if you did, you could have more assurance of salvation. Nobody really talked explicitly about the guilt code. It's not like a cross-stitch reference list hung on the wall in the church lobby. Nobody wrote the code down on the back, blank side of a business card to refer to throughout the day— at least, as far as I know. But if you hung around long enough, you could learn the guilt code. It was just in the air we breathed. It went a little bit like this:

- If you're worthy of the "free gift" of salvation, you'll prove it by living a holy life.
- Lesser sins, like gossip, doesn't disqualify you from receiving heaven.
- If you sin, your salvation is in jeopardy.
- Habitual sin separates you from God. You're responsible for repairing that relationship.

The guilt code had amazing powers to produce obedience—well, at least until you popped your next boner or heard a couple of beats of secular music. Most folks in my church growing up lived the guilt code. That sucked for the average high school student. They were constantly bombarded with temptations. But in my estimation, I was an outlier. I was the youth group kid the parents trusted. Let's just call me the King of Youth Group.

I still abided by the guilt-code approach to Christian living and looked good on the outside. At least I wasn't falling into sin that was easily observed by outsiders. I wasn't drinking beer at parties, sleeping around, or telling dirty jokes. I was just dying on the inside and afraid of hell. Things may have been dark for me, but at least I was a shining glimmer of hope to other parents of students in the youth group.

Chapter Four
BROKEN TABLE, BROKEN PROMISES
——

When I was sixteen, I used to work for a guy who owned an art gallery. One summer, my boss moved his art gallery from one location to another. Two of us were assigned to move all of the furniture. I was carrying a glass shelf and accidentally banged the corner against the inside edge of a doorway which caused part of the corner to chip off. Not the biggest deal, I reckoned. For all I knew, the shelf wasn't even going to be reused. Maybe it'd be thrown into a recycling bin.

Not. So. Fast. Suddenly, a gnawing feeling grabbed the pit of my belly, and my face got hot and flushed. I knew right then and there that I was falling into a web of obsessive no-win, no-way-out thinking. I needed to tell my boss what happened. I had to tell him, "Because of my carelessness, I accidentally chipped your shelf. I'm sorry." But maybe he'd think that was silly? I mean, for the love of God, the chipped side of the shelf could be placed on the inside, up against the wall, when the shelf was hung again. It was no big deal. But wasn't it a big deal if I didn't just come clean and be honest?

Coming Clean with the Boss

I imagined a spiritual enemy had launched an elaborate plan against me. I was being made to obsess over something trivial, and tormented for lack of honesty. When I felt that rush of panic, it only took the moment of getting into my unreliable Oldsmobile Cutlass Sierra for the drive to the new gallery location to know I was down for the count. It was sinful of me to keep the chipped shelf a secret, and it would be weird to call my boss and tell him about it.

Joey: Hey, sir.

Boss: Hey, Joey. What can I do for you?

Joey: Yeah, I know it's probably not a huge deal, but when we were moving your stuff yesterday, I accidentally chipped a small piece of glass off the corner of the shelf. I just wanted to come clean about the incident.

Boss: Oh. Thanks for telling me. It's no big deal.

Then I imagined him putting the phone down and thinking to himself, *What a good kid. That's a bit weird though for him to call me about a tiny thing like that.*

It felt too awkward to make the call. At that point, I'd convinced myself I was under no compulsion to do so. My anxiety was silly. Until the next day, the life verse came to mind—James 4:17, for those taking notes. This was a devastating blow. At that point, I'd felt silly to call my boss about something as insignificant as a piece of chipped glass. But I had to. Otherwise, I was in danger of hell. I knew that telling my boss was the honest thing to do. I shouldn't have kept it from him in the first place. I'd finished moving all of the furniture. Now I was under moral obligation to come clean.

Of course, I knew that Jesus had taken away all my sin. I'd pretty well taken care of the authentic Sinner's Prayer conundrum, but the "sins of omission" were different—you know, the sin of not doing the right thing, which was my sin. So I just needed to do the right daggum thing. Then, that sin could go away. But it wouldn't go away because the sin of not doing it was there as long as I hadn't done it. You see, with sins of commission (i.e., doing bad things), I couldn't take it back, nor do anything but ask for forgiveness. Sins of omission? I was caught in a damning cop-out. I couldn't just ask for forgiveness without making it right. And, this wouldn't go away until I made it right. Eight months after the glass tabletop-chipping fiasco, I was still obsessing over it. I had to call my boss. Sweaty palmed and cotton-mouthed, I dialed the number.

Joey: Hey, sir.

Boss: Hey, man! Good to hear from you. How's school? What are you calling for?

Joey: Yeah, I know this is going to come across as kind of weird, but remember last summer when I helped you move?

Boss: No, we still live at our old address. Oh, you mean the gallery! Sure, I remember. What about it?

Joey: Well, when I was helping you move, I carried a glass shelf out to the car, but on the way, I accidentally banged it against the inside edge of your door and chipped a piece off the corner.

Boss: Oh. OK. So why are you telling me this?

Joey: Well, I just wanted to say that I'm sorry for my carelessness and for not telling you sooner, and I'm willing to pay for the damage.

Boss: Joey, that was a long time ago, but I don't really care about any of this. Are you feeling OK?

Joey: Yes, I'm feeling OK. So you officially forgive me, then? There's nothing else I can do to make it right?

Boss: Joey, I'm going to hang up the phone now, OK?

Joey: Wait, I just want to make sure that . . .

Boss: [Click.]

The above conversation actually never happened. I eventually wised up to my mind's trickery, and embarrassment won out. I realized I couldn't muster up the courage to make the call and had to let it go. I was pretty sure I'd dodged a bullet and averted hell this time around. But in other situations, what if a mistake I made caused someone else to burn in hell forever? I could never let that happen.

Chapter Five
ROLLER SKATING HELL
—

This is a story about a crush—well, a girl I was crushing on, who unfortunately was on her way to hell. It all started on November 1, 1993. I remember the date not just because I was obsessed with a girl, but I was obsessed with dates. I couldn't help it.

The fall of 1993 was an important time. My grandfather, whom I was very close to, died. My brother shipped off to college three-and-a-half hours away. Our family started going to a different church than the one I grew up in since the fourth grade. Yes, sir, a lot of change. I can't forget that year.

But the exact day in November? Well, it happened to be one year re-moved from the date of asking a high school sweetheart to go out with me. "Going out" just meant talking on the phone, saying "hi" face to face, and holding hands every now and then. I'd gotten acquainted with this girl among friends at a youth group hayride hang out night. Things had gone well. She thought I was hilarious, and well, she was cute, so coupling up was a no-brainer. A second "date" was in order, so I took her to Christian Skate Night the following Monday. We would end up having a conversation that would climb into my brain and plague me for a full year.

Christian Skate Night

Christian Skate Night involved no secular music and no bad kids. It was all good, clean fun. Though the rules weren't official, they were fine-tuned. As an example, it was common knowledge that when a kid was seen wearing a Guns N' Roses T-shirt, it basically meant that they were destined for hell. Christian Skate Night was a statement. The DJ was going to crank up those Newsboys and Stephen Curtis Chapman jams. We'd make sure the hoodlums knew that even if it was only one night, we owned the place and weren't going to take kindly to unbeliever or backslider shenanigans.

At first, we'd planned on Christian Skate Night being a double date, but my buddy canceled on his date. The reason? I'd called him up earlier and told him that my date and I were going alone. I'd pulled off the perfect sneak-attack dating tactic—a strategy I'd later use at least a couple of times in college. It was just me and the girl of my dreams. Smooth. When I pulled into the driveway to pick her up, I told her our friends had canceled and it was just the two of us. Oh, man, you could tell she was beside herself with excitement. This was my first official date. This was the real deal. I was growing up. I was moving on to bigger and better things. I was driving a girl around in my car and paying for her dinner. You know it.

We were destined for a perfect night, but then she mentioned that she disagreed with something that my youth group leader said. You see, this girl was a once-saved-always-saved Baptist. But I was a Pentecostal boy; things were different on our side of the tracks. Sure, you can get saved and have the joy of the Lord in your heart while you're out on a Sunday drive. But if you get cut off in traffic two minutes later, you've got to keep your cool. If you lose composure in the moment and give that guy the middle finger, veer into traffic head-on, and die in a car crash, then, well, you'd burn in hell forever and ever. That's just how things were on our side. Being a part of our crew wasn't for the faint of heart. You had to keep your salvation tank full at all times.

Once Saved Always Saved? Hell No

She mentioned that she had heard my youth pastor say that we had to keep our end of the bargain with God or we'd lose our salvation. She disagreed and asked me what I thought. I don't remember exactly how I responded. I'm sure I had a real buttoned-up doctrine of salvation up my sleeve. But a few days later, I realized I hadn't articulated my position well enough. I couldn't sleep. I tossed and turned, knowing in my heart I hadn't done everything to save this girl. She believed a pagan doctrine, and now hell awaited her, and it was my fault.

Now I had two problems. I couldn't be forgiven until I made things right with this girl, and her blood and burning hot body—no pun intended—in hell was on my hands until then. Not only did this girl have a major flaw in her doctrine, but I was in no shape spiritually to pursue a romantic relationship if I couldn't adequately refute her position. It sucked. She was really pretty, and I think she dug me. But there would be no second date. I ignored her until she got the hint.

Internally, I was a mess, but I was convinced I was hearing from God. Couldn't I just date a hot girl and enjoy daggum high school, for the love of everything decent? Nope. Souls were at stake, including mine if I didn't get and keep my act together. Eventually, we got back to an awkward hi-and-bye friendliness when we'd see each other in the halls. I felt bad, but there was nothing I could do about it.

Save Yourself

A whole year passed, and I was still losing sleep over not confronting her faulty, baptistic theological position. There was some unfinished business to tend to. I had some truth to drop. Of course, you could lose your salvation, duh! How could she be so dumb? Of course, it wasn't merely her stupidity; the enemy was at work. And it was time for me to put my fundamentalist superhero gear on and go to battle. I wrote her a letter. It was the perfect plan. I wouldn't have to strike up an awkward conversation with her and wouldn't feel humiliated to revisit this year-old conversation. I'd just send a letter about deep spiritual truths to a girl I never talked to but once went on a pseudo date with. Of course. There was no other way.

I think it was September 1994 when I wrote the letter. I acknowledged the weirdness of how strange it might seem to get a letter from someone she was in chemistry class with every day. So I cut to the chase to point out her bad theology. I proof-texted a few verses and explained how I was responsible to tell her this. And of course, this had nothing to do with why I never asked her out again. "I just wasn't ready for a relation-ship," I said. And we weren't well matched anyway since she believed in cheap grace.

I dreaded going to class that next day, but I got there first. I reckon that was best and would be more comfortable for both of us. She stiffly walked right by me to her seat. Whether she attempted eye contact or not, I'll never know. I sure wasn't going to look at her. No way, José. The humiliation and discomfort was well worth getting the gorilla-sized burden of her damnation off my back. It was done. I was a weirdo, but at least she wasn't going to go to hell on account of me.

Chapter Six
THE GIRLFRIEND
—

I've been delusional about many things in my life – fearing hell for not saying the Sinner's Prayer just right, failing to witness to friends at school, and disobeying speed-limit laws. But it also included my love life—like believing God's will for my life involved marrying a girl I had no romantic feelings for. Somehow, God made good out of my delusions. Had I not been convinced of this, I wouldn't have gone to Winthrop University. I wouldn't have met my best friends. Most importantly, I would have never met my wife, Pricilla. It's kind of a chicken-or-egg thing. Did God make me crazy to get me where He wanted me to be, or did He just deal with my craziness as He worked His plan? I may never know.

So this girl. I met her at church, and she was incredible. She had a great personality. She was funny, talented, and she really enjoyed spending time with me. She was maybe the first person outside of my family who really got to know me super well and was still a big fan of mine. In no time, we were pretty inseparable. We were self-identified best friends, and we planned to get married. Oh, and I totally wasn't into her romantically.

Shortly into the relationship, once we defined the relationship as "more than friends," I recognized that I wasn't in love with her. I had no butterflies or anything. And yet, I was convinced that she was the one for me. Crazy, right? Well, this is a book about my craziness. We had plans to get married right out of college, so it just made sense that I would follow her to Winthrop University.

The Dream Team

So the plan was in place. We were both in Rock Hill, South Carolina. Four years of Winthrop University and we'd be husband and wife. Everyone knew us as a pair. We were together all the time, and we all shared the same mutual friends. And yet, I still wasn't into her. Keep in mind, this was a time when I wasn't quite right in the head.

Like the time she and I were in the car with our friends to go do something fun. Out of the blue, I just got it in my head that I had to be by myself, right there and then. I could have said, "Hey guys, I'm sorry for the inconvenience, but I'd really like to be alone. Can you take me back?" Instead, I got out of the car at a traffic light without saying anything and walked home alone. Or how about the time I said something stupid, and my girlfriend and best friend started making fun of me. I erupted in anger, stormed out of the room, and rode my bike through a sketchy, unsafe part of town.

I was acting strangely around my friends. And for some reason, I was also convinced that I was supposed to marry a girl I had no feelings for. I was convinced God had spoken. We were supposed to get married. Because of that, I was supposed to have romantic feelings. And the fact that I didn't was my fault. Until I could muster up enough faith in God's love for me, not only would I not be rewarded with clarity in life, I would be at risk of spending eternity in hell. All I needed to do was figure out how to truly believe, and the feelings would come. Then we'd enjoy our happily ever after. In the meantime, I felt completely justified in pretending that happily ever after was in the here and now.

One night, my girlfriend and a few friends were watching It's a Wonderful Life, and my girlfriend's roommate lamented about a particular romantic scene as something that happens only in the movies. I told my girlfriend that I disagreed with her roommate's sentiments. After all, we had that romantic happily ever after. I was forcing it. It had to be true. This part of my life had to be in place. We were supposed to be together. We were supposed to be in love; otherwise, I had nothing to hold on to.

Failure to Fall in Love Equals Lack of Faith

I could have come to the sensible conclusion that I didn't have feelings for this girl and needed to break up with her. Instead, I concluded I was falling apart because of my lack of faith. Life was becoming harder because I wasn't doing my share in believing. So I decided to hit the irrational decision button. I convinced myself that it wasn't God's will for me to be in this relationship after all, but also came to the conclusion that if we were married, it would automatically become God's will for us to stay together. So I made the suggestion. One night, we were on the fringe of falling apart, and I actually said, "I do want to be with you. Let's just get married right now. Let's open the Yellow Pages, find someone who can do it, get married today, and have sex tonight." Sex would have fixed everything. She wasn't so irrational or hasty. To this day though, if she'd been game, we would have gone through with it and gotten married. And that would have been quite the predicament, because I didn't believe in divorce, either.

Praying in My Dorm Room

I remember one night trying to figure out my dating predicament. Intense prayer was the answer. It had to be. Faithful, on-fire Christians have to go after God. While my roommate was away at class I'd lock myself in our room and pray my guts out. I believed that the more passionate I was, the more serious God would take my prayers. I would pace back and forth in my room, cry out for God, pray for friends and family, and pray that God would reveal himself to me and fix my messed up dating life.

My belief in prayer is that any time we reach out to a loving Father, there's good fruit borne. When my child comes to me with a silly request, I feel like we can at least laugh about it and get a hug out of the deal. Can anything bad come out of going to God in prayer? Probably not, but if so, I think I certainly teetered toward it with my mental assent to prayer. It was a vicious, helpless cycle.

In reality, I was depressed and chemically sick. That's why I thought obsessively about marrying a girl who wasn't "the one." That's why I kept a piece of paper hidden in my desk drawer that said "you asked for salvation" with check marks beside it. Little did I know that two years later I would uncover a world of depression I had been living in for years.

Chapter Seven
PENIS ANGUISH

—

Life-long trouble. That's what my dang penis has caused me. I don't mean that in the garden-variety, Christian-purity complex sense. Compared to my neurotic obsessions, conventional moral guilt would actually be a relief. As I came of age and had a couple of dating relationships before meeting my one and only, Pricilla, my penis anxiety started ramping up. I planned on being a married man after all, and we all know what that means: sex. But sex meant I'd have to eventually show my future spouse my penis. That was a terrifying prospect. But my penis fears began way before I had my first dating relationship. I can trace my penis ails all the way back to one fateful shower.

When I was little, sometimes my dad had me step into the shower with him. Maybe to conserve water or time, I don't know. Now that I think about it, I was probably too dumb to effectively clean myself. I can't remember my exact age, but I'm guessing it was 1985, when I would have been in third grade. Dude, learn to clean yourself already.

Awaiting My Own Wangtastic Wiener

Needless to say, every boy at eight years old has a little penis. Fortunately, no one at that age cares. Then you get into the shower with your dad. My Lord, when the giganticness is unveiled from behind the curtain, it's mind-blowing. To a young impressionable mind, observing an adult penis is like looking at a completely different body organ than the one you're accustomed to. An adult penis might as well be an alien appendage. It's like the difference between a straw and a garden hose. The difference between one of those itty-bitty appetizer sausages and a Coney Island foot-long. To an eight-year-old mind, the way a Tootsie Roll could metamorphose into a serpentine monster is a confounding, horrifying mystery. At least it was for me. The image was permanently etched into my mind. I was haunted.

When would I get my Wangtastic Wiener? All I could do was wait with excited expectation for my new and improved penis to magically appear. It was a long wait.

Well, years went by. I went through puberty, and unbeknownst to me, my penis had indeed grown. But growth is relative. Your feet grow in relation to your legs, in relation to your arms. I reckon the same must have been happening down yonder, too. But to my young mind, I imagined waking up one day to man-sized hugeness, getting up out of bed in the morning, standing up to stretch, and seeing your protruding wiener knock over the alarm clock. The big, magical penis was on my mind continually.

Rites of Passage

This reminds me of how obsessed my kids are with losing teeth. To them, it's a sign of maturity, growing up, and keeping up with their peers. You never know when it's going to happen, but when it does, it's a joyous day. There are occurrences leading up to getting "snaggled." Feeling the teeth wiggle and seeing others experience the same thing is a rite of passage.

The rite of passage for me growing up was getting hair under your arms and 'down there,' talking about sex, and growing a big schlong. When I was a kid, I was losing teeth like crazy. That was no rite of passage for me. I was waiting for my huge wiener to appear. Every time I peed, I was reminded of what I didn't have and what I was waiting for.

I waited and waited. The magical penis day never came. By the time I was twelve, I started to get nervous. In my pubescent ponderings, I wondered if my experience was anything similar to how a preteen girl experiences getting her period. One day, no blood in the undies; the next day, boom! Likewise, one morning I'd wake up, and 'boing,' a big, strapping, adult-size penis. It would be awesome. I'd tote that package around with pride like it was a pet. I'd finally have a bulge the wimpy kids would fear and the chicks would dig.

So I waited. And waited. The longer I waited, the more I feared being stuck with a mini, forever.

Boys' Room Bragging

I'll never forget in middle school, I was shoulder to shoulder with another kid taking a whiz in the urinal next to me. He was yammering on about growing into adolescence—like there was some kind of award for pubic growth or something. He said, "You know, it's no big deal. You just get some hair under your pits. Grow a big dick. Grow some hair on that. You know, no biggie. Whatever." He gave the old three-jiggle pee shake, snapped his undies, zipped up, and flushed—ka-shhh—like it was some kind of mic drop or something. I'm still not sure who he was talking to. As I zipped up, I scanned the bathroom. It was only me and one other kid washing his hands at the sink.

It was like he was talking to himself, but for the benefit of everyone fortunate enough to listen in. Maybe he was admitting to himself how small his penis was. I may never know. Either way, that trivial locker room monologue confirmed my penis fears. Looking back, my plumbing functioned as designed to factory specifications. I peed straight and always woke up with a boner. All was well. But the penis shame loomed over me.

The Micro-Penis Confession

When I was about twelve, I became friends with a kid in youth group who was a couple of years older than me. He admitted to having a micro-penis. We were standing in the children's church lobby, just the two of us, waiting for our parents to come pick us up. What was weird is we never played video games together, and he'd never been to my house. Back in the early '90s, these two things were prerequisites for close-friend consideration. If we'd played *Super Mario Brothers* together at midnight while eating Little Debbie snacks, I suppose a micro-penis confession would be in order. But video-game-snack-time-friendship warm-up be damned. He told me anyway.

I was there for moral support only, but hell would have to freeze over and polar bears skate on the once lake of fire for me to admit to the same fears. At least, he wasn't alone. His friend also struggled with his tiny prospect. He told me they'd both get so depressed that sometimes they'd sit in silence at the thought of being shortchanged on the day God was handing out penis-growing ability. I remember listening to the sob story myself and thinking, *Shoot, this is me, too. I'm in the same situation.*

I don't know for sure if that kid was truly cursed with a micro-penis or if he just obsessed the way I did. Lucky for him, things turned out in the end. To this day, he has a healthy marriage and some kids to show for it. So either he was lugging around penis-size shame like me, or he put his micro-machine to work. Good for him.

How I Broke My Wiener

The second major building block of penis-induced fear and shame came from the first time I masturbated. For years I looked back on this as one of the worst mistakes of my life. I won't go into all the details, but I wonder if other guys have a similar story. I saw all the fellas jokingly act out the jerking-off hand motions as a way to poke fun at their buddy. I heard all the terminology. I remember one guy pick up a pole during recess, bring it up under his groin, do the hand motions, and scream, "It's coming! It's coming!" I didn't get it. *What was coming?*

At the same time, I was flipping twelve years old. Like millions of other twelve-year-old boys, we all felt the pressure of being jacked on hormones. Thoughts of girls would flash uninvited into my brain. I'd get all flushed during make-out scenes in movies, and I'd awkwardly flirt with girls at school. All of these experiences led me like a sheep to the slaughter to that night in my living room while my parents were away. Yup, I started playing with my own daggum self. Experiencing that for the first time was like, wow. It can't be put into words. But you guys know what I'm talking about. A year or two of marathon masturbating, and fear of my small penis size continued growing. To my young mind, my self-taught jerkathon experiences were the biggest mistake of my life. Before proceeding, readers, beware. We are now officially entering too-much-information territory.

WARNING

Did you really want to keep reading?
OK, I gave you fair warning. For the rest
of you, skip ahead a few pages.

Marathon Jerkathon

So there I was, with a solid two-year career of masturbating under my belt, and things began to change. My ejaculations had become more significant. I was confused. That dreadful first day of masturbating had only produced a very small amount of semen—one small drop to be exact. But what did that single drop mean?

Since I'd started emitting more of my seed, I figured it was the proper way the body functioned. But since that didn't happen the first time, I must have masturbated too early in my sexual development and shut off my body's capacity to grow a bigger penis. I thoroughly believed my own reasoning and was tortured by it.

I figured my body must have thought to itself, *Well, the penis can now function in an adult-like manner, so it must be adult size, now. Time to shut off the growth factory for the reproduction system. Our job is done here, boys. Let's clock out and go home.* But the job wasn't done. It wasn't! I needed a way to talk with the Senior Hormone Secretor in charge and get things straightened out once and for all. I needed a bigger dong! Please, Senior Hormone Secretor, don't stop now!

As middle school turned into high school and high school into college, I was plagued by small-penis fear. I imagined eventually getting married and on our honeymoon my wife thinking to herself, *What have I gotten myself into?* She would tell me through angry tears, "Damn you, Joey. What in God's name have you done to me? You've been dishonest with me all of these years! I would have never married you, had I known. God in heaven, help me!" All I could do at that point was hope I was wrong. Penis growth had stopped, and there wasn't a thing I could do about it.

Every year I'd get a physical examination. You know, the whole turn-your-head-and-cough thing. All those years, I never got the I'm-so-sorry-Joey-but-you-have-a-micro-penis talk. I hung out with guys and would jokingly come out of the shower into the dorm room naked. No one said anything. If my friends and my doctor weren't going to level with me, I figured, maybe my parents would.

Snail-Mail-Penis Picture

In my freshman year of college, I remember reading my biology book on the top bunk and coming across a description of a sexual development disorder both males and females were susceptible to. I think it was as simple as testosterone and estrogen shortage. Two adolescents were pictured separately. The girl had broad shoulders and no breasts, and the boy had a small penis, small breasts (that were blacked out, despite an uncensored penis) and narrow shoulders. My heart sank. That dude's problem was my problem. Small penis. There was no solution.

My life basically ended that day. The hope of future sex was at the center of my world. But my hopes had been dashed on the rocks of low testosterone production. I couldn't face the humiliation alone. If my calculations were correct, I needed someone else to know. If I was wrong, I needed someone to tell me that, too. Who could I share this embarrassment with? Well, it wouldn't be easy, but I had only one option: my poor, dear parents.

I rode my bike to the library, made a copy of the photos from the biology book, got back to my dorm room, and wrote a letter to my parents explaining my predicament. I wrapped up the letter, along with the Xerox copies, and walked down the street to the mail drop with a great sense of relief. I shoved that dang letter into the slot and listened to it "ka-thunk." Knowing there was no backing out was a great sense of relief. Someone else would know my fear. I didn't have to suffer in silence anymore.

The response from my parents was anticlimactic. I reckon it was normal. I mean, I had great parents. What could anyone say to their crazy son who sent them pictures of a testosterone-deficient penis from their freshman library book? My mom and dad called, and I'm pretty sure my dad was silent. I don't recall much about the conversation other than my mom saying, "Joey, I'm sure you don't look like that guy pictured. Joey, he has breasts. You don't have breasts. And I'm sure your penis doesn't look like that." Thanks, Mom. I can always count on you to make me feel slightly less inadequate about myself.

Since the penis-inadequacy incident, every so often my parents would drop subtle hints that maybe I struggled chemically with depression and obsessive, irrational thoughts. Maybe I ought to go see a doctor and get on medication. But they were dumb. What do caring parents who have 30 years more life experience than me actually know?

Seeing Is Believing

Fast forward six years later and I was engaged to get married! But time was ticking. Soon I'd find out whether my wife would have the dreaded "WTF" honeymoon moment I'd been losing sleep over. The moment I'd take off my pants on our honeymoon night and she'd look down at my penis and say, "WTF, how is this going to work?" For full disclosure, my wife and I got married before having intercourse, but it's not like we were superhero saints either.

Our premarital escapades ended quickly because, first of all, Pricilla and I were balls of raging hormones begging to be let out, and because we weren't comfortable (out of guilt) to relish the moment and enjoy ourselves. If anything, it was, let's do this before one of us gets convicted or acquires some supernatural willpower and ends this sexual ecstasy. Because of this approach to our premarital sexual relationship, I could never be comfortable with what she thought. As far as I was concerned, I was still in the dark with whether or not I was good to go. And it was becoming too much for me to bear. I began hinting to my parents that I was getting nervous about the most important night of my life.

I asked my dad to go to the other room and sat him down on the couch. I explained to him my predicament. Then, with no other choice before me, I pulled my elastic athletic shorts down and looked at him for approval.

"Is this OK?"
"Yeah," he said as he patted my knee.

I want to take a second and tell you something endearing about my wonderful parents. My dad was just certain I was going to open up about my fear of having sex for the first time. He solemnly and seriously started with, "Son, on me and your mom's wedding night, what we did was . . ." *Dear Jesus, no, Dad! Please, Lord Jesus, no! Thank you, though. I'm touched that you were willing to go there with me.*

Anyway, I can't begin to tell you how relieved I was to hear that. Thanks, Dad! But I wasn't out of the woods, yet. The fear of having irreparably damaged my goods due to early life masturbation didn't let up until my wife became healthily pregnant. Even when we started taking part in good old fashioned sexual intercourse, I still feared sterility. Four kids later, the plumbing seems to be working just fine. No problems there. Now I'm the father of two sons, and everything has come full circle. I was in the shower recently with my two little fellas, and there we were—two baby minnows marveling at their dad's big, gigantic water snake. To them, I'm like the Seventh Wonder of the World, just like my dad was to me.

Chapter Eight
PRICILLA
——

It was time to come out of the depression closet. It was a cool day in Charleston as I walked to the mailbox and dropped in my letter. A few days later, my future wife, Pricilla, would walk out into the frigid weather in Iowa and retrieve a letter from yours truly. She didn't want labels on our relationship, but I hoped my letter would change that. At the very least, it would give her a lot to consider.

I dropped the bomb. The fascinating dude she was hanging out with had a hidden dark secret: depression. I cryptically wrote, "Miss Pricilla Halvorson, Joey Svendsen isn't perfect. Despite the vibe he so naturally gives off, you've been duped." I'm not sure why I wrote to her in third person. I guess I was trying to create fascination.

Pricilla told me later she paused to reflect on what she was getting herself into. Did she want to take the relationship further with someone plagued by depression? There was no way to know what future hurdles and pitfalls were ahead. I'm glad she thought I was worth taking a chance on. I must reluctantly admit this hasn't been the easiest road because being married to me isn't without cost to her.

The DTR Moment

Over time, we gradually defined our relationship. We had something special. My second trip to visit her in the Midwest helped us take a more official stance on being some sort of "couple." She was staying with her aunt and uncle in Minneapolis. One night we were in the living room watching a movie. The day before was a full travel day, and I was tired. We were watching a boring movie, so I kept falling asleep. I was in a daze that night, but one thing led to another, and I made my move. We kissed for the first time and had, oh, I'd say about a 45-second or so make-out session—tongue and everything. It was pretty much perfect. Movie-scene material, if you know what I mean. But we were cautious to not let our hormones take control and decided to call it a night. Pricilla was scared and resisting the relationship moving too fast. She hadn't planned on getting into a serious relationship. Too bad she met Mr. Irresistible Killer Kisser. But we didn't want to mess things up. So it was goodnight. I'm pretty sure after going to bed, I considered revisiting our make-out fireworks show, but I got over that quickly and went to sleep.

The next morning, I packed up my things, and she took me to the airport. Our short weekend together had come to a close. As I folded up my clothes, the clouds rolled in, and an internal war began. I began doubting we'd kissed the night before. I'd been so groggy the night before, maybe I'd only dreamt it. But if I'd dreamt it, why didn't I remember how I got into bed? I had to confirm the happenings of the evening somehow.

I couldn't come out and ask, "Did we make-out last night?" That would be too bizarre. So instead, I, the pansy that I am, said, "I can't believe that happened last night." She simply smiled and touched my arm. Dang it, an arm touch wasn't enough. I needed her confirmation that the make-out fireworks show was real.

On the plane ride home and the month following, I didn't know if our kiss was real. We talked on the phone, I sent her bizarre emails. "Wow, it's like that never happened." But no matter her response, I couldn't be sure we'd kissed. For 45 seconds. Maybe I was like Russell Crowe in A Beautiful Mind. Maybe she didn't even exist. Wait, maybe I didn't exist! Nah, I wasn't that crazy. The definitive answer never came. But after our third make-out session I realized that first kiss had happened after all. Why that cleared things up in my mind, I don't know.

Taking the Relationship to the Vertical Limit

Things were going well in our relationship. On our fourth visit, Pricilla came to Charleston for five days, and I was presented with a whole new brain challenge.

I picked Pricilla up from the airport and I'm telling you, she gave me one of the best hugs of my whole life. Man, being in love—there's nothing like it. I was living with my parents for the summer so she crashed in my brother's old room. We had spent lots of time together before, but not for this extended amount of time, and not without friends and family around for the majority of it. Everything was awesome. Until Saturday night, when it turned into a nightmare.

We were watching "Vertical Limit." It was like Sylvester Stallone's "Cliffhanger," except teens were doing the mountain climbing. Pricilla was completely zapped. I asked her if everything was OK. She sleepily said, "Yeah, everything's OK." Well, yeah, of course, everything was OK. She was having the time of her life with her favorite person in the world. She was getting to know her awesome future in-laws. But something about her tired response meant my worst fear had come true. *"OK"?*

What do you mean "OK"? Don't you mean "amazing"?!

That was it. She didn't want to be with me. Her eyes were saying, "I don't like you anymore, but I don't have the heart to tell you while we are watching this intense mountain climbing thriller."

Later that night I went to bed and wrote in my journal, "My worst fear has happened. It's over." I cried myself to sleep. I woke up in the morning convinced I'd stumbled on the truth that she didn't want me anymore, and the rest of the weekend dragged on. Eventually, I got over my fears, and things got back on track. But there was always something lingering in the back of my mind. I had to seal this deal, and quick.

Pricilla Moves to SoCal

Later that summer, Pricilla would be moving to Southern California. She was not planning to end our relationship, but she wanted to have some new life experiences before jumping into an engagement. But that idea was worthless to me. If she didn't want to be with me for good right then and there, I figured just break it off and call it quits. Before I took her to the airport on our last day together, I tried to get her to admit that it wasn't worth sticking it out. In my mind of black and whites, if Pricilla wasn't willing to get engaged with me right away, we'd be better off just throwing in the towel completely. But Pricilla went to California anyway, though it was short-lived.

Our plan was to get officially engaged during her Thanksgiving visit to Charleston, but Mr. Slick had surprises up his sleeve. Now, being slick, I was naturally a creative and funny person. The sky was the limit with the different ways I could have popped the question. But I was fixated on one thing: dates. We had to get married on a specific date. I had to propose in August. It was August 31st, and time was running out.

August was my birthday month, but most importantly, it was the month we'd be married the following year. To my mind, it made complete logical sense that the day of our engagement would be in the same month.

I've never had any regrets about marrying Pricilla. She is my one and only. I just regretted how I rushed popping the question. I could have proposed on Venice Beach on one knee. I could have taken her to Hollywood. I could have tripped and pretended to break my leg only to hold out the ring when she reached out her hand to help me up. Instead of doing the research for a cool place or brainstorming a fun, unique, and romantic way of proposing, my Rain Man mind was focused on numbers. It had to be done in August, and time was running out. So there we were, sitting in a California airport parking lot on a Labor Day weekend, the sound of jet engines overhead. I proposed right then and there. I have to admit, writing this bums me out. But hey, it's been 15 years. Happy anniversary?

Chapter Nine
SEXLESS HONEYMOON

It was August 2, 2002, and I'd just married the love of my life, Pricilla. The Emery dudes attended the wedding and had gone through the motions of wedding attendance, throwing flower petals at us. But I could tell they were jealous. Jealous I was now officially married and a few short hours away from having sex.

I was a virgin. I'd like to say I waited and kept my penis to myself because I loved Jesus and wanted to honor Him, and I loved Pricilla and wanted to honor her. I reckon that's a small part of it, but those things weren't motivating enough for me to make it that long. If I'd been so concerned with honoring God and women, I wouldn't have crossed the lines in sexual sin with Pricilla, stopping shy of sex. We messed up, felt bad, swore we wouldn't mess up again, but you know what? You guessed it. We messed up again. One time, we felt so guilty and ashamed, we decided to stay apart and not see each other for a few days.

The Churchy Stigma of Premarital Sex

In the church, losing your virginity before marriage is hyped up as a sin that will destroy the chances of having a healthy, married sex life once and for all. Sex outside of marriage is an abomination to God at the highest level. Well, it's a sin just below cursing and having attractions for the same gender, of course. Premarital sex is something to avoid at all costs. The only problem here is that most Christians have had sex before marriage, and they usually fall into one of these categories:

1. They are still happily married.
2. They claim healing from their past sexual sin.
3. The sexual sin they committed with their soon-to-be spouse is now a distant memory.
4. They are divorced for many reasons beyond having sex before marriage.

You don't run into too many people who say, "We got a divorce. It was ugly. We should have never had sex before marriage. That would have solved everything." Or, "I'm still married, but our sex life sucks. Should have never had sex before marriage."

Do I believe it's good to avoid sexual sin? Of course. Do I believe that it can benefit the intimacy of two people if they save themselves for one another? Sure. I also believe we can be blessed by doing things God's way. But if God blesses people only when they live up to their end of the bargain, we are all royally screwed.

Here are the facts: Pricilla and I never had sexual intercourse. But the healthiness of our sex-life was hampered due to past sexual sin, as well as the challenges of my mental illness. Here's the point of the backdrop to my honeymoon story: The church needs to grow up a little bit, stop singling out "sexual sin," and look at some of the deeper issues. Issues like:

1. Selfishness is more threatening to one's marriage

and sex life than previous sexual sin.

2. Avoiding sexual sin altogether is leaps and bounds more valuable than avoiding intercourse. Sometimes we feel like moral badasses for avoiding "intercourse," but we know daggum well we don't have anything to be proud of. Let's do away with the we-only-had-oral-sex ridiculousness.

3. Many good marriages exist even when one's past involves many sex partners. God can bring good out of all things. He redeems stuff, remember?

4. Those with rough marriages are affected negatively by many issues beyond sexual promiscuity.

The truth hurts, but I'll say it: Some of the healthiest married couples I know have had premarital sex. Some of these couples were even promiscuous leading up to marriage. I'm not promoting promiscuity by any means. I'm only encouraging Christians to see sexual sin in a different light and to stop focusing on "different levels" of sexual sin. If you've had a bunch of oral sex with your partner before marriage, you're not better off for not having had a bunch of intercourse.

I've known many people in desperate need of healing from past sexual mistakes (and harmful sexual acts done to them). But I've also come into contact with many in need of healing from the love of money, drug addiction, bad spending habits, and pride.

So you get the picture. I had nothing to be proud of and yet I felt like I deserved a badge of honor for holding out sexually. I was a good guy for saving myself and deserved applauses from heaven. King David burned with jealousy. I mean, you know what that jerk did. As it turns out, I was the most self-centered, self-absorbed, self-serving guy imaginable. But remember, Pricilla and I never had intercourse. So I was still the good guy.

Wedding-Week Stress

So there we were in the hour-long limousine ride to Cedar Rapids from Cedar Falls, Iowa. We would fly out the next day to our New England honeymoon destination. But let me back up a bit so you understand the emotional state of my wife at that moment.

Pricilla's parents divorced when she was young. Typical of most divorces that involve kids, there were many conflicts and heartache between the adults. This included the complication of remarriage and strained family dynamics. All the pain that comes along with divorce is a lot for a kid to navigate. Unfortunately, that process doesn't end in adulthood.

The heartache and complicated relationships followed us right into our wedding week. But I was too self-absorbed, immature, and oblivious to appreciate the emotional toll all this took on my fiancée's heart. But hey, I was just shy of 25. I thought I had nothing else to learn in life. In reality, I was barely out of kindergarten in the school of the real world. Pricilla has a huge heart, and it overflowed with love for Mom, Dad, Stepdad, and Stepmom. She's also eager to please and do everything she can to make everyone comfortable and happy. Our wedding week should have been a time of happiness. But despite the rehearsal dinners, first dances, and the big walk down the aisle, it was impossible to keep everyone happy.

As for me, I was in heaven. My best friends in Emery had arrived in town a few days before the wedding. My best friends from South Carolina were there, and my beloved family traveled halfway across the country. I had no work obligations, and the people I loved the most were all around me. I was getting married to the girl of my dreams, and I was going to have sex by the end of the week. I didn't have a care in the world. I was oblivious to the burdens that came along with Pricilla's family dynamics. A "typical" wedding week is stressful for any bride. And everyone was vying for Pricilla's attention, and she wanted everyone to be happy.

Later, I was shocked to learn that wedding week had been so hard for Pricilla. Beyond enjoying the emotional escape of our ceremony, everything else was really hard for her. Right after the ceremony, she was sucked right back into the stress of wanting everyone to be happy. By the time the meal, music, hugs, toasts, cake, dancing, drinking, and celebrating commenced, my wife had emptied herself emotionally. She had very little to give.

At risk of sounding cheesy, Pricilla needed the guy who loved her most to reach out with some tenderness and understanding. She needed her heart filled back up so that we could begin our blissful, one-week honeymoon on Squam Lake in New Hampshire. But all I could see was that I was next in line for her undivided attention. I needed her to please me sexually. And in my mind, this was nonnegotiable. It's what people do on their wedding nights, right? And looking back, my nearsightedness, self-centeredness, and horniness screwed everything up.

I've beaten myself up a good bit for this. But you know, I was young and dumb. I just assumed that Pricilla was ready to party. She was super attracted to me, and during our engagement we had to work really hard to postpone the party.

The Honeymoon "Party"

It didn't compute that our wedding night would be one of the most emotionally and physically vulnerable nights in my wife's life. I was completely unaware of how intricately connected sexual intimacy was to a woman's emotions and state of mind. Go ahead and laugh if you want to. I was in my fourth year of study at the School of Pricilla, and I'd spent most of those years skipping class. I didn't even know this girl. Those of you who have been married for more than a year know exactly what I'm talking about. People think they know the person they are marrying. But we usually have no idea. A decade later, we'll still be scratching our heads saying to ourselves, "What the hell did I just say to make her so mad?" Or, "Why in the hell did she not like that present? I thought it was perfect." Or, "When the hell am I going to learn effective communication with this complicated alien from outer space I call 'spouse'?" But 14 years ago on that honeymoon night, I had no idea who Pricilla was.

But, hey, it was my honeymoon night. After all, my dad said "I was good to go" for the big moment. Unfortunately, I was incapable of processing anything in the world through any other organ than my penis. Yes, sir, young and dumb. Put Joey from 2016 back in time on our honeymoon night and I would've easily had that girl floating, my words lifting her delicate spirit, my hands knowing exactly what to do. I would have been the loving, attentive husband, and we would have ended up having some amazing sex. But like the biggest dumbass in the whole world, I wanted to skip the talking and caressing and start having sex, like, yesterday already.

There we were in the limo. I remember thinking, "Heck, we can do anything we want right now." God's rules weren't stopping us anymore. I didn't have to hold back—as if I didn't have to honor my wife anymore. I seriously started to make moves right there in that limo. I thought to myself, we could either go all the way right then and there, or at the very least, we could get loose, show out, and cross some unchartered territory. Then we'd be desperate to check into our hotel room. But she didn't respond to my advances. She wanted to freaking talk? You. Have. To. Be. Kidding. We've been talking for the last four years. I was done with the talking nonsense. It was time to get it on. You heard that Marvin Gaye song. Those lyrics might as well have been blaring in my head:

I've been really tryin', baby
Tryin' to hold back this feeling for so long
And if you feel like I feel, baby
Then come on, oh come on

But someone wasn't feeling how I felt, baby. Someone wanted to connect emotionally first. She needed to talk about her feelings on her wedding day. From my vantage point—at the time—she might as well have punched me in the face and told me she hated me. Rookie Husband Joey was just put in the game and was fumbling big time. I was throwing interceptions, goal-tending, traveling, and striking out in the blink of an eye. But I was pissed. There was no way it was my fault. She knew what I wanted, and she was being selfish as hell to put her feelings before my sex drive. Who did she think she was?

But I rebounded quickly. I took her reticence to mean she didn't want to fool around in the limo, but that she needed to calm down from the stress of the wedding. But then when it came to the hotel room, it was party time. But what she was really saying was, "I need to talk this out. I need you to pick up on some clues here and be interested in where I'm at in my head. Try to connect emotionally with me." But like I said, I was blind.

So we got to the hotel, and I was like a kid waking up on Christmas morning to see what Santa left. I remember leaving the room to get some ice or something. I was probably skipping with a smile on my face. If people saw me, they would have thought I was high or I had just won the lottery. But it was better than that: I was about to lose my virginity on my wedding night.

I got back to the room and little by little began making my advances. Remember, I was oblivious to her need for emotional support. I sensed her hesitancy once again, and if there's such a thing as an unforgivable sin of blaspheming the horny husband, she had committed it. I was pissed. I saw her as the selfish one. She finally had to spell it out and say, "I'm not ready! I'm an emotional mess." Those weren't her exact words, but you get the picture.

If Pricilla said this to me in 2016, the scenery would be beautiful, and there would be a lot of sexual optimism. Nowadays, if sex isn't going to happen, I'll get a clear "no." But "I'm not ready. I'm an emotional mess"? That means "I want to party. I'm just not ready." You'd better believe I'd know where to go from there.

But 2002 Joey's response to Pricilla not being ready was basically, "OK, not much I can do for you, selfish girl. You get ready, and in the meantime, I'll sulk, feel sorry for myself, and reflect on your selfishness." Joey, 2002 wasn't your best year. You just didn't get it. The night started looking better, but still, no sex. I'm pretty sure I didn't give her the floor to explain all of her emotions. Maybe she did. I'm not sure because I wasn't paying attention.

Sexless Honeymoon Depression Sets In

The rest of the honeymoon had minor highlights, but for the most part, it sucked. I was already struggling with depression. And as you'd expect, not having blissful, intoxicating honeymoon sex, a night I had been anticipating my whole life, sent me spiraling down pretty hard.

Over time in our vegetarian, un-air-conditioned bed-and-breakfast, we were able to talk things out. By the way, the hot tub was not in private quarters, and the couple managing it were weird as living hell. The lady actually tried to sell us her crafts before we left. It was a miserable place to live for the week. Thanks for the shrimp and grits and bacon and eggs, you hippie weirdo. You're a shady saleswoman who is beautiful and loved in the sight of God. Thanks for the public hot tub, which did wonders for our honeymoon sexcapades. OK, I'm finished venting. This rant was 14 years in the making. Bless my little heart.

Throughout the week, Pricilla and I fooled around a little. But I was so depressed and traumatized by the emotional toll that the first night took on me, it wasn't all that enjoyable. For the most part I had problems—ahem—performing. This was devastating. Outside of the few bright spots, our sex life started on the worst, crippled, bunion-covered foot in the history of the world. My irrational thinking immediately decided it was the ineffective antidepressants I was on. I'd come all this way with my "dad-approved penis" that was either in the way or always getting me into trouble. And now those little bastard antidepressants weren't going to help me be happy, and were robbing me of the only thing I cared about in the moment. Peace out, antidepressants. I stopped taking my medicine cold turkey. Anyone with any experience with medication knows, you have to taper off meds gradually. There's always the chance of severe side effects, like having a seizure behind the wheel of the car. But given the choice between a car crash and sex versus erectile dysfunction? It was an easy choice.

Chapter Ten

FISH OUT OF WATER

—

OCD and Depression

The current medicine wasn't doing the trick. Dopamine and serotonin regulator, my ass! The only regulated thing was the doctor visit. I knew what came next. The doc was just going to say, "Increase the dosage." Surprisingly, the rug gets pulled out, and I'm being told brighter days are not right around the corner. I have to start a new medication. Again. Increasing the dosage isn't safe. So the doctor firmly hits the medication reset button, and I have to start over. It's going to take time to kick in. And I have to wait to start. Meanwhile, I obsess over the litany of possible side effects. I can hear the end of the commercial in my head.

"If you have moderate-to-debilitating, batshit-crazy depression, Depress-B-Gone may be right for you. Side effects are uncommon, but may include headache, nausea, vomiting, death, dizziness, vaginal ejaculations, dysentery, cardiac arrhythmia, mild heart explosions, varicose veins, darkened stool, darkened soul, lycanthropy, trucanthropy, more vomiting, arteriosclerosis, hemorrhoids, diabetes, virginity, mild discomfort, vampirism, gender impermanence, spontaneous dental hydroplosion, sugar high, hourly yearnings to snort white lines in

public restrooms, even more vomiting, brown, your mom,
and mild rash."

Sweet. I'm really looking forward to that mild case of potential constipa-
tion and death. Between 1998 and 2004, I tried 'em all: Prozac, Effexor,
Abilify, Lexapro, Buspar. Sometime between Prozac and Effexor,
I took Paxil. Three weeks into it, I experienced a depression-less day.
The euphoria of having that bad boy lifted is inexpressible. But the next
day that sucker just nestled his way back into his familiar home. I reckon he just took a day off. Welcome back, depression! Take a load off,
and have some sweet tea! Would he leave again, maybe next time on
a permanent vacation? Nope. Would I have to try a different medicine?
Yes. I was fed up, unwilling to take the torture any longer. Eventually,
the pain and fatigue of constantly seeking a solution wrecked me.
By 2001, I gave up. I couldn't do it anymore.

Two years passed, and I didn't take any medicine (you remember what
those a-holes caused on my honeymoon), but Pricilla thought it was
time to revisit a pharmaceutical solution. She wanted me to at least try.
If taking medicine made my wife happy and it wasn't hurting anything,
I'd do it. But honestly, I didn't care either way. I'd been depressed for a
while with no relief. If I got better, great. But I wasn't counting on it.

More Adventures in Medication

All the doctor had to do was pick a new medication I hadn't tried. Eeny,
meeny, miny, moe—Zoloft it is! Here's your prescription. The doc went
through the rigmarole. Four days of Zoloft, and I started to feel relief.
I didn't get my hopes up. I'd already been punked out by Paxil years
prior. *Why you gotta be so whack, Paxil? Never again, antidepressants.*
But with Zoloft, the clouds kept lifting. I could see clearly now. The rain
was gone. Rational replaced irrational. Lightheartedness outweighed

heaviness. Excitement overcame boredom. Happiness squashed sadness. I couldn't believe it. It felt like I'd been crippled but suddenly could walk. My mental load lightened, and it brought a smile to my face. For months I'd been obsessed with getting enough sleep. But now I didn't care. It may seem inconsequential, but I felt like I was a fish washed ashore and was safely in water again. I was living a life I never knew I could live, and I did nothing more than pop a couple of pills.

Hello Again, Depression City

Not quite. My fish-back-in-the-water experience lasted a few weeks, but things started to digress. Before long, I was laying out on the dock on that sketchy pier, down in Depression City, and flopping around. After meeting with my doctor, he determined I needed a one-two punch of meds. One for depression, the other to treat OCD. Zoloft and Wellbutrin to the rescue! If there were such a thing as a prescription skills game show, my doc would have kicked everyone's ass.

There are days I feel fine. I'm not weighed down by depression. OCD isn't making my mind run 1,000 miles a minute. I look forward to the day. I'm not easily rattled. But the next thing you know, I'm leveled, stuck on the dock in Depression City again. Sometimes I can track how I get there, sometimes not. Every so often, a thought picks a fight with me and beats me down. My brain throws punches at me like, "Hey, you hear about that case of whooping cough going around? Yeah, it doesn't matter if your kids got immunized." "How are you ever going to retire? You better up those savings, son." "Yeah, some pastor you are." "Boy, you're one great husband."

But sometimes I have no idea what just happened. All I know is, everything is negative and I'm back up on that dock gasping for air, and the storm clouds roll in. There's nothing else I can do. So I wait it out, knowing the storm won't last forever. I may be wrong to see it this way, but I haven't found a solution. Sometimes, the storm passes after a few hours. Other times, it settles in for two to three days and doesn't come back for a month. These days, depression comes three to four times a month, one to three days at a time. You do the math.

How OCD and Depression Set In

I'm typically detailed-oriented. I feel responsibility for the details of life. This can be a good thing, making me dependable. But sometimes, my sense of responsibility for the legitimate and illegitimate details of life get tweaked. This can easily get out of hand, and before you know it, I'm staring at a salvation checklist, convinced I'm going to hell.

As I try to figure out the relationship between my depression and obsessive thinking, it seems as if the same chemical condition leading me down the path of OCD is paired with the same feeling I get when I'm unhappy. The feeling for both is the same. It's a sort of throbbing, burning sensation. I don't know if depression causes obsessive thoughts or vice versa. They typically seem to go hand in hand, but this isn't always the case. I've also experienced times of feeling empty and numb, but my mind wasn't racing in a million different directions. All this to say, I don't understand how my mind works. And for those of you who are plagued with OCD and depression like me, you're not likely to understand it either. But sometimes another person's perspective can help. Sometimes.

The Blind Date That Saved My Life

Do you remember the first time someone else put words to what was going on in your head, and helped you identify the reality of your mental illness? Maybe a doctor, a pastor, or a friend showed concern.

My parents had been dropping hints about my depression for years. When I had OCD episodes or was spiraling into depression, they could hear it in my voice and see it in my eyes. One instance in particular stood out.

Back in the day, my brother and future sister-in-law paired me up with a girl they worked with at a coffee shop. They hyped her up big time. She was pretty, funny, smart, witty and interested in meeting yours truly. That's right, baby. It was official. I was going out on a blind date, and I was excited! I wondered to myself, Maybe she'd want to make-out on the first date (which I'd find myself repenting for later, I'm sure). Maybe our first date would lead to more dates. Any mystery date is exciting, but when a reliable source like your brother officially deems your blind date as hot, it makes the rest of the mystery especially exciting.

Later that morning, my brother called me to give some unexpected news.

> "She's not going to be able to do it man. Sorry," he said.
> "Hope it's not that big of a deal."

There was no explanation. He didn't say, "She wants to do it another time." It was just a simple, "she can't make it." I think what he really meant was, "Sorry, Joey. Against our better judgment, we showed her a picture of you. Worst mistake ever." "No, man," I replied. "No biggie."

As I said those words, I was sincere. It wasn't a big deal. I had nothing invested in it. I had high expectations for the day, but that's no spilt milk to cry about. As I hung up the phone, I sat there on my cheap Goodwill sofa and pondered a bit. And then I fell hard. I crashed. The black storm clouds moved in, and I fell into a deep, dark depression. Suddenly, it dawned on me. A canceled blind date was really no big deal. There was no rational reason why I should feel depressed, and I knew better. Why couldn't I just shake the immense sadness? I thought, Holy crap, my parents were right—I was clinically depressed.

My Parents Finally Bust Me for Depression

I called my folks, explained my discovery, and they both simultaneously burst into laughter, "Ahh, told you so!" They laughed hysterically. They mocked me by fake crying and cracked depression jokes at my expense. Thanks, guys. I really appreciate the heartfelt, sincere response. All joking aside, we did have a constructive conversation and talked about what next steps might look like for me. It was time to get medical attention. This started a tumultuous six-year process of trying different medications in different dosages before I finally found something that tweaked my brain into a functioning state. Finally, some relief.

Experiencing Depression Is Like Being a Fish Out of Water

I'd been lugging a form of depression around since I was a kid. It'd ramped up in high school and college. I'd subconsciously just accepted it all as just a part of life. To finally realize that I had depression was like a fish realizing it's not in water. That poor little fella—we'll call him "Billy Bass"—couldn't conceptualize the invigorating life of swimming and receiving oxygen through the gills until someone threw him into the ocean. Until then, I'd been "lying on the dock," trying to take in air and live normally. I'd been on the dock for so long that I didn't realize there was anything better. I hadn't been metaphorically thrown into the deep blue sea, so I couldn't grasp what it felt like. I could get some relief by just knowing, unlike some stupid fish on the dock being told eye to eye, "There's a better life for you. You belong in an ocean. You are supposed to breathe better. You can actually move.

It's called swimming."

Depression and OCD Are Not Easily Understood

Fast forward a decade-plus, and as I write this, I wish I could tell you I never struggled again. I've had a lot of ups and downs since, some of the downs exceeding anything I experienced prior. You'd think that twelve years of this crap would also bring about complete understanding of why I struggle with it, what causes it, and what the most effective tools are to combat it. There are, indeed, many aspects of my struggle that I understand a lot more than I did then, but there's still a lot more understanding to gain. I've had to learn a balancing act between being OK with it, and wanting to grow, fight, and learn more through reading, receiving counsel, and listening to general feedback from my friends' and family's observations.

Some of you depressed folk reading this have been wrestling with shame and self-condemnation. No good comes from this. In actuality, you are adding the needless pain of negative thoughts about yourself onto the pain that's already there. Don't you think the mental illness causes enough pain for the day? Now you have to go and add more to it by beating yourself up? I can call you a dummy because I struggle with depression, too. I'm just a smart depressed guy.

Chapter Eleven
SO YOU KNOW A CRAZY PERSON. NOW WHAT?
—

This chapter is for the mentally healthy folk. Congratulations, you're not crazy. But your loved one is. Bummer for you. You didn't ask for crazy, but here you are. Your significant other, your pal, your partner in crime is nutso in one form or another, and let's just face it, it's not always easy doing jujitsu with crazy.

The fact is, millions of people struggle with mental illness. Now think upon the multimillions of friends and family connected to old nutjob. Yup, that's a whole lot of people relationally neck-deep in varying levels of crazy. And it can be crazy making. Am I right? It's not often said, but as you try to be a helpful support, it's painful for you. There are expectations put on the supportive party, and it's tough.

On the ground in real life, there are seasons of our married life where Pricilla doesn't know which Joey she'll get from day to day. The unknowns can be scary. We've been through times when depressed Joey walked through the door after work. I'd go through the motions until the kids went to bed, then I'd crash without even saying good night to Pricilla. This has been hard on her, my family, and my friends alike.

Depression Affects Family and Friends, Too

If you're walking alongside a depressed loved one, remember this: If you've never experienced clinical depression firsthand yourself, there's no way you can fully understand the experience. But still, you're supposed to be understanding, patient, and kind. Not only that but you have to find the missing puzzle pieces of how to act when the storm clouds descend. Then there are times when Crazy Town wants you to leave them alone altogether.

The fact is, those of you connected to a depressed person are thrown through the ringer in one way or another, too. Hang in there. This is hard work for everyone involved. But if we can come to an agreement early on, I think we can all learn from one another.

If you are a supportive loved one wanting to help a depressed person, this is for you. If you can keep your cool, approach the topic of mental illness with humility and a desire to learn, not a posture of assumptions or quick fixes, we can get somewhere. Willingness to listen and learn is the first step.

And for those facing depression: Yeah, your spouse, friend, coworker—they don't understand what it's like to suffer depression. But they're having a difficult experience as someone who loves and cares for you, too.

I want to outline what my personal experience of depression is like. I'll give you a glimpse into what a day in the life might look like, and then reflect a bit on what I've learned about what I think is happening behind the scenes. I'll also reflect on how I try and coach myself through depression, and aim to avoid what tends to trigger my depression. Lastly, I'll give some advice as to what to say, and what not to say to a depressed person. So, you ready? Things are about to get interesting. Buckle up kids, cause we're going to Crazy Town!

A Day in the Life of My Depression

One day, I arrived at work super early. I had just spent some time in prayer and was gearing up to listen to some hip-hop on the way to work and do some writing. I kissed my wife and daughters goodbye. My heart was warmed as I thought about my family on my commute. I stopped by Dunkin' Donuts and practiced dietary discipline by averting my eyes at the donut counter. I even stuck with cream only for my coffee—no sugar! Not a care in the world. This day was basically like any other day. Sure, I still had unanswered questions in my life like we all do. I had challenges to figure out and trials to endure. It's just that the everyday weight of the world wasn't weighty. I felt tough as nails and ready for the day.

But that's just a snapshot of a moment. The complete story is that I was in hell the previous night. I'd finished a productive day's work, and my beautiful wife was ready to hang out and relax. We could have cut up, laughed, and had a grand old time together. Instead, I climbed into bed, plagued by a tidal wave of thoughts. I'd secretly indulged in obsessive overeating and didn't feel well in my stomach, and I felt guilty about it. I worried about finances. I was tortured by the thought that friends and coworkers looked down at me, and I was struggling to endure unanswerable spiritual questions. I had it in my head that my wife didn't care about what was important to me. In short, the weight of the world was crushing me.

Seven hours later and I was "Mr. Joe-Joe on the go-go, who was happy for sho-sho." No life changes had occurred while I was sleeping. It's not like I'd just learned the Green Bay Packers won the Super Bowl last year instead of the New England Patriots. I simply woke up with a properly functioning brain. My wife got the fun-loving husband, my kids their goofy but understanding dad, and my friends their witty, lighthearted, cut-up-all-the-time Joey. (Boy, I'm quite the catch!)

Out of nowhere, I had just lost perspective. My perception of life wasn't true. Why didn't I know there would be light at the end of this irrational tunnel? Don't get me wrong, in the moment I realized I was depressed, but I was hooked on the thoughts that were making me depressed. It's hard to properly evaluate a situation when your brain is the problem. Unfortunately, the waves of depression often come unannounced and at all the wrong times—like when your wife is planning a surprise birthday party for you.

Partying with Depression

I'll never forget my 38th birthday last year. I was going through a very difficult time, and I'd completely shut my wife out. I know this makes me sound like a complete a-hole. But I can assure you, when I am depressed at this level, I'm not flippantly thinking, *Since I'm depressed, I think I'll make my wife's life hell today.* When depression rolls in at this level, I feel paralyzed. The thing is, this social paralysis is magnified when I'm around people closest to me. So yeah, it was one of those days. Happy birthday to me.

So Pricilla called me into the kitchen and through sobs told me she had invited dozens of people over to the house for a surprise birthday party—exactly what I didn't need that day. But the look of pain in her eyes devastated me even more. She was doing what any loving wife would do for her husband on his birthday. Fun-loving, cut-up Joey would have loved the party she'd planned. But not today. Instead broken-brain Joey had moved in for the day unannounced and was about to wreck the party.

Sometimes Depression Comes out of Nowhere

I've had plenty of sunshiny rainbow-in-the-distance, Clemson-Tigers-are-national-champs kinds of days, and all of the sudden, Bam! The clouds roll in out of nowhere, and my mind starts scrambling, *Oh, crap, what thoughts caused this? What practices can I do that the psychologist taught me?* But there's nothing I can do because I realize the depression storm isn't tied to anything I can discern. I can't untie myself from triggers that don't exist or ones that are successfully beating my tail in Hide and Go Seek. I can't find solace in telling myself the truth because there's no lie to correct. I suppose it's possible that there's always a cause for my depression. But when the depression comes out of nowhere, I can't pinpoint the hidden triggers. Oh, the complexity of my crazy brain!

This is why talking to my psychologist has been helpful. On the one hand, he's given me helpful practices to equip me to deal more adequately. He acknowledges my chemical imbalance and the helpfulness of medicine. Medicine doesn't always have to be a depressed person's first go-to, but a trained psychologist can help you sort it through. While you're doing what you can to overcome depression, sometimes medicine can help clear the air and give you a head start. Figuring out what works is often an investigative, trial-and-error process, so be patient.

Depression Is Like Emotional Smoke

Depression isn't a poor reaction to life's curve balls. It's more like emotional smoke that causes poor reaction to life's curve balls. It's like two firemen that run upstairs to save two kids' lives. Once upstairs, one hangs a left to save Johnny. The other hangs right to save Sally. The major difference is that the fire is located on Johnny's side of the house. Sure, both firemen end up running the same distance to the rooms on opposite ends of upstairs. They will both need to use their firemen expertise to save another person's life. Both take the same precautions and prepare for the worst. But the fireman rescuing Johnny will have the tougher challenge because of the smoke that keeps him from seeing clearly.

Someone with legitimate chemical imbalances in their brain isn't just handling life poorly, but is dealing with real physical challenges that are just as obvious to them as smoke is to firemen. To clarify, I don't think a depressed person is a helpless victim. There are proactive steps we can take to get rid of the smoke. But those steps are typically pretty complicated and rarely 100 percent successful. But I'd even say that sometimes the metaphorical smoke that we call "depression" can be avoided altogether. This is a tough truth that I'm reluctant to admit. Depression can sometimes be avoided? Yes. I didn't believe this until recently. This is often hard to detect and a truth that can often be difficult to discover given how natural it is for our bodies to react to destructive thoughts. At least in my case, not only is it hard to detect when a thought begins to take a negative toll, my chemical downward spiral can also go unnoticed.

It's Hard to Understand "What's Happening" with Depression in Real Time

Are you still with me? Are you making an effort to understand? For those of you who are, here's another curve ball. We, the depressed and anxious, understand a lot less than we think. Yes, we've experienced depression, and we can describe how depression feels. But so can someone with chronic stomach problems. It takes going to the gastroenterologist to understand the cause of why you're on the verge of exploding in your pants at the most inopportune time. There's a major distinction between going to a doctor for a physical ailment and going for mental illness.

When you get a checkup with the gastroenterologist, he's going to tell you something like this: "Well, the reason you almost shit yourself at the most inopportune time is because you have a stomach bug. There is a virus attacking your stomach lining that's causing this sensation." If the patient has a healthy brain, they'll understand, nod, and say, "Ah, yes, the Pants-Shitting Syndrome. It all makes sense now." But in the case of depression, things are different. A key factor of depression is an operationally impaired mind. We depend on the mind to process information and make sense of the world. Imagine what happens when you're depressed. The doctor might say something like, "Well, Joey, it looks like your depression may be related to an imbalance of natural chemicals between nerve cells in the brain. I'm going to write a prescription that will work to correct this imbalance." Those words go into my ears, get translated by my broken brain, and I'm unable to accept what's being said. My internal response goes something like this: "Whatever, Mr. Psychologist. Nice Zoloft commercial, but can't you see the sky's still falling, dummy?!"

You see, in the moment, my mind is impaired, and I'm handicapped in how I process information and see the world, including how I process my depression. But after putting some psychologist-recommended exercises in place, I've begun to put some reps in. It's a gradual process, but I've slowly learned some coping skills that seem to help, a few notes to self that I've rehearsed.

I Might Be Dead Wrong about Depression

In the meantime, I'm open to being wrong about depression. I've been seeking God and professional counsel on this issue for twenty years and haven't settled my convictions 100 percent. I'm a stronger person for having gone through this, and it brings me back to the sufficiency of Jesus and His grace. Whether I'm right or wrong, I'll concentrate on pointing to God's glory by swallowing my pride and talking openly about my depression. He gets to be the hero for helping me through. I'm no hero. Don't tell my kids this, though—they pretty much think I'm Captain America.

I can't figure out if my depression is God's intended purpose, and I guess I don't care. I can't assess an infinite God using finite measures. All I know is that being an open book about my depression has comforted and benefitted others. I don't have all the answers, obviously. All I can say is, I'm pretty sure Jesus is the answer for all depressed and non-depressed people, Christian and non-Christian people alike. He's the dude, the hero for everyone. Maybe one day we'll all be surprised about just how heroic He is.

A Word to the Spiritual Giants Who Know What to Do about Depression

Rule No. 1 for those who think they have answers for the depressed person: Know that I can't just "snap out of it." When someone tries to tell me to snap out of it, I'll probably tell you to snap out of having an ugly face. OK, really, but for someone like me, this kind of comment isn't helpful. Don't ever assume a depressed person is slacking on troubleshooting their problem. Remember, depressed people are mentally and emotionally crippled and may not have the strength to do what is obvious to you. Instead, have some grace.

As a professing Christian—someone who is supposed to sing proudly, Victory in Jesus, my Savior forever—there's certainly been some confusion for me through the years regarding my depression. Spiritual 'cheerleaders' will come alongside me from time to time to give some "encouragement." These folks love cutesy bumper sticker statements like the following:

- Just believe and receive healing from God
- You aren't praying enough
- Resist the devil and he will flee
- Persevere
- The battle has already been won on Calvary
- Let go and let God
- By his stripes, you are healed.
- His pain, your gain
- Turn right or get left
- Your boss is a Jewish carpenter

And the list goes on. For the record, these truth bombs aren't helpful. All smart ass-ery aside, though, it's hard to admit, but your "kind"—you turbo Christians, you cheerleaders for Jesus—are needed in the church. Many of you have the gift of faith. You believe in God's goodness more than the rest of us, and when you pray, you do so with the expectation for answers. That has to be a good thing. When I'm around people like you, I'm encouraged.

But I hate to say it—a person with this kind of faith isn't typically balanced with the key ingredients of wisdom and understanding. Often those with the gift of faith often have an extra helping of religious dogma on the side. This causes genuine fear in the face of God's mysteries. You like black and white. You prefer to connect the dots. You like to put things in boxes. I get that, but the Bible that you use as your box says that God can't be put in one.

In the meantime, together maybe we can acknowledge the mystery of a God who loves me but hasn't healed my depression. Who knows why? I know you want to give an answer. But please practice self-control, and maybe we can both walk together into some unknown territory, knowing God loves us and is for us.

Aside from the spiritual cheerleader types, there are those who have a brass-tacks, logical, pull-yourself-up-by-your-bootstraps mindset. I know these people mean well when they say, "You have to take responsibility for your depression." But it doesn't help. Sorry.

14 Ways to Help a Depressed Person

Lots of people are affected by one's depression. The supporting characters, the friends, family, spouses—they want to understand. They want to help. If you're in a supporting role, you may be asking yourself if there's anything helpful you can say or do. As the concerned love one, it's hard, isn't it? Yes, your depressed loved one is in pain. And it's painful for you, too. What can you say or do that might help? If you relate to this, then this section is for you.

I'm going to leave you with 14 quick bits of advice that may help as you interact with a depressed loved one. This is based on my personal experience, and no two depressed people are the same. But when the time is right, ask if any of the following would be helpful.

1. It's usually difficult to talk about depression when I'm depressed. I think the main reason for this is that the conversation typically brings added guilt knowing I negatively impact those I love. Ask, does it help to talk about it in the moment? Ask if I'd like to talk instead of forcing me to. If I'm not too low, I may be willing to.

2. We're on shaky ground when we invest our stability and contentment in another human being. No fallen person can be your savior, whether they're depressed or not.

3. Your depressed loved one isn't intentionally trying to hurt you—I hope. For me, I have to try and resist feeling bad about hurting those I love. If I wallow in hurting others too long, it makes me more depressed and, in turn, may not benefit you at all.

4. Try not to resent your depressed loved one. We're only human. Resentment happens. But ask yourself, would you be more sympathetic to someone if they got in a bad car accident and were forever paralyzed?

5. Talk to trusted friends about depression. Find someone you can talk to openly about walking with someone with depression.

6. Say something nice. I know it may be hard, but a kind word goes a long way. It takes a lot of pressure off and could help lighten someone's day and aide in getting your loved one the heck out of the darkness.

7. Don't allow yourself to get into fix-it mode. When someone has the flu, they need to be willing to do things to get better, but you wouldn't expect a quick fix. When you're sick, sometimes it takes a while to recover. Your demands for solutions aren't helpful in the now.

8. If your loved one remains unwilling to seek help, ask someone for advice, maybe even a professional.

9. Remind yourself that your loved one is hurting.

10. Everyone has to take responsibility for their meanness and irritability. But these are also part of the sickness. The brain moderates our behavior, and when it isn't functioning in a healthy way, it follows that behavior may be unhealthy as well.

11. Ask, "Do you want to talk about it?" Don't ask incessantly, but do ask once a day.

12. Before you leave the house, ask if they want to come. It may be hard for a depressed person to take initiative to be included, but it's likely easier to say "yes." If you ask and they say "no," try not to get mad. It won't do either of you a bit of good.

13. Ask if they've thought about self-harm. To ask this question shows that you recognize the serious nature of the pain associated with depression.

14. If you are the praying type, ask God to give you strength. Lean on the strength of God for your own sanity. God works even in counterintuitive ways. Sometimes when we are at our limit, we have no other option but to turn to God. And situations that cause trust in God are a great gift.

Chapter Twelve
GOD'S GRACE IN DEPRESSION

—

I've got a whole lot of memories related to my OCD and depression, but my time in college really stands out. The irony is, it involves times of intense prayer. I can remember times of being in deep depression but not realizing it at the time. That's the thing: sometimes you don't always know that you've got it until later. Weird, right? But I knew something was off. My spiritual tank felt empty, so I prayed my guts out in my dorm room like I talked about a couple of chapters ago.

My daily dorm room prayer time became a ritual. I figured the more passion I squeezed out of my prayers, the more likely God would listen. I paced the room like a whispering Pentecostal preacher (I couldn't let the neighbors hear me after all). I cried out to God for friends and family, and asked that He'd reveal Himself to me; that He'd deliver me from my darkness.

To reach out to our loving Father through prayer is always good. When one of my kids comes to me with a silly request, we can at least laugh about it and get a mutual hug out of the deal. Of course, only good can come out of going to God in prayer. But I may be the only person you know who can take a wonderful thing like prayer and turn it into a problem.

Depression had set in. I was sick in the brain. I lived in a world where I obsessed over coming up short. For the love of God, I kept a paper reminder in my desk drawer that read, "you asked for salvation" with a bunch of check marks on it. It was a miserable predicament, and my sick brain was the culprit.

But how could prayer be a problem? Easy—prayer had become about earning, and earning counters the entire gospel message. The good news of the gospel is the center of the faith that I run to in desperation. But at the time, I was worlds away from understanding it.

I set out to seek God. That's good, right? Sure, but not when the misery I felt daily was tied to a lack of faith. And when my prayers were primarily used to get more faith from God. I figured with more faith, my pain would subside. And yet, the pain I was trying to ease by drawing closer to God was physical. My brain caused the pain, not spiritual mishandling on my part.

Depressed at Birth Plus Fundamentalism Equals Hellfire

I may be wrong, but I believe my problem started at conception. If only there'd been in vitro Prozac, maybe my pathetic OCD and depression could have been avoided. The fact is, some people are predisposed to struggle with OCD. So, no Prozac drip in the womb. As if the predisposition toward jacked up brain chemicals wasn't enough, add legalistic fundamentalism to the mix. I was screwed. It was hellfire for me.

As I'd mentioned earlier, when I was about eight, my parents had a life-changing encounter with Jesus. For whatever reason, they decided Catholicism was no longer for them. We stopped going to mass, and started attending Pentecostal churches. We kept this up for a good ten years. The problem was, Pentecostal churches were bent on preaching the "gospel" in a way that scared the bejeebers out of me. Though the message was scary, I embraced their teachings. I not only embraced them but practiced their version of piety in an off-the-charts unhealthy way. I was going for the gold, baby. The Christian of the Year Award would be mine. All mine. But I'm not letting the Pentecostal, holy rollin' folk off the hook completely. Some of their teachings are nuts. But I was nuts, too, and took the bait.

I'm also convinced, for the most part, these brothers and sisters were well intentioned. They were genuine believers. They were just passing on the old-time religion of their parents. No one knew any better. They had genuine salvation through relationship with Jesus. It's logical why they couldn't recognize their unhealthy spiritual paradigm.

The messages I received in these churches were the only messages this community knew. My obsessive, rule-following, people-pleasing, compulsive, irrational-thinking heart found a match made in heaven. Turns out, OCD and religious legalism is a beautiful pairing; and it made for a complete disaster in my soul.

My Good Pal "Scrupulosity"

There's actually a psychological term for my obsessive praying. It's called "scrupulosity." It's a form of obsessive-compulsive disorder. A disorder characterized by Jonathan Abramowitz in a CNN article as a "fear of sin or punishment from deities."[1]

In the same article, one woman had concentrated so hard on praying for

[1] http://www.cnn.com/2014/05/31/health/ocd-scrupulosity-religion/a

forgiveness, she'd block everyone out. She said, "First, I had to get rid of all my sins, ask for forgiveness, do it in the right way, and then I had to pray for protection. If something bad happened to my family, it would be my fault because I had not prayed good enough."

I can relate. In the Super Christian Club, if you sin, you're on shaky ground. Super Christian Club offers no guarantee of salvation. One's salvation was always in question. Big bummer. Because maybe I had committed a sin without knowing it, or I had sinned by failing to do what I knew was right. Super Christian Club made spiritual life impossible.

Here's what this meant in real life. Let's hearken back to my days as a teenager. Remember the driving-to-school story? Let's change it up a bit and instead of flipping someone off and losing control of my temper, let's just replace it with having a lustful thought. Let's say I'm driving myself to school and I happen to have a lustful thought. But then out of nowhere, a runaway bus comes careening around a corner. There's a horrible wreck, and I get all mangled up into the dashboard and die. What happens next? Well, I go straight to hell, of course. There was no time to ask for forgiveness. Boy, what a God—one who is wringing his hands looking for his lucky chance to send me to hell. Thankfully this God is not depicted in the Bible.

The True Heart of God (He Likes to Save People)

Over the years, I've learned that the God I believed in actually wants to save me. It took me a while to learn this, though. You see, Christian faith is about putting faith in Jesus, not in ourselves. That's the whole point of needing a Savior, right?

But I used to think God should give me some sort of miraculous sign, like speaking to me audibly. I'm not sure why He doesn't speak to me audibly. I've heard He does that with people. That's messed up, God. What about me? You like Benny Hinn more—even though he lies to people? (Oops, don't print that last line, Mr. Editor.)

Although some claim otherwise, I don't hear God calling in the plays of my life. "Next play, check your e-mail, visit your grandma, and then rest. After that, the plan of attack will be to spend time with the kids. Oh yeah, I want you to check the mailbox as soon as you get home. It's important that you do that." God talking me through a checklist of to-dos is the last thing this OCD player needs. I don't need to ask God about the details of every aspect of my life. Dear Jesus, no. I'm skeptical when people claim to relate to God this way. I could be wrong.

But there are times in life that involve major decisions where I feel God spoke loud and clear; times I've felt directed and guided. Other times, God spoke—at least, I'm pretty sure He did—to steer me in a different direction.

Here's one of the most significant things God wanted me to know: He actually wanted me. It's a simple concept I've always believed "on paper" but not in my heart. Had I believed this simple truth, I wouldn't have walked on eggshells, constantly asking Him the same daggum thing. This is the most significant spiritual change I've made in my head over the years. I believe it represents the real God.

If He created humanity to receive His love, this has to mean something simple. Ready for it? He actually wants us to receive His love. Boom! This was an epic shift in my thinking. But I didn't understand this for years. My false understanding that God was trigger-happy, ready to send a lightning bolt down on my head at a moment's notice, was at the root of my obsessive prayers for forgiveness.

Before coming to this understanding, I believed God wanted to save me. He knew I wanted to be saved, but if I screwed something up, there was nothing He could do. He'd lose me for eternity, and it would be all my fault. That's one weak, pansy God. This led me to a life of constant "correct prayer." But I was never convinced my prayers would ever succeed. This cycle repeated itself again and again until I came to the realization of what God's response was to me: "Dude, I know what you are trying to say. The answer is, yes, I will save you. You just asked—23,345 times, to be exact. Did you forget I can even read your mind?"

This new revelation of who God is was major for me, something that many people can take for granted. Upon discovering this theological jewel, there were bonuses, like logic. I realized salvation isn't something I got based on my request. God accurately reads my thoughts because he's omniscient. So the concept of me trying to ask for salvation was impossible. I wanted to talk to God. He's everywhere, so He heard me. I wanted salvation. He knew that's what I was asking for, and He heard. Slowly but surely, I started getting used to following a God who wanted me. It was a gradual process, but peace started settling in.

I know, this stuff is elementary to most people. But it's not elementary to a sick mind locked on a warped view of God. These were things I had to learn. I also recognized there was no possibility to win the battle of my obsessive prayers. I could never say them perfectly. And if I did, it was only a matter of time before I would doubt the legitimacy of them altogether.

Salvation and Imperfect Faith

I also had a drastic shift in how I viewed faith. For the longest time I saw faith as a work that I needed to fine-tune. But all through New Testament scripture, I read that salvation was received through faith, and our faith is imperfect. But I never heard this as the true blessing that it was. So I'd think to myself, "OK, so all I need is faith. I have to do everything I can to have that. Then, I have to make sure I've done everything I can to know that I have it."

Instead, maybe the faith I could have was the same saving faith portrayed by the guy in Mark 9. The man that desperately needed his son to be exorcised from a demon. Jesus wanted to heal his son and said, "Everything is possible for those that believe." The dude's response? "I believe, but help me with my unbelief." Then, boom! Jesus released the boy from the demon's power.

Think about the flip side of this. The person who utters this kind of prayer isn't looking to keep a death grip of control on their life. That kind of person wouldn't be praying things like, "I want to believe!" Once I realized this about myself, a calmness settled into my spirit. The truth that God has known me my whole life, knew all the thoughts and doubts in my head, and knew my intentions. Most important of all, He knew that I wanted him. If the God of the Bible was true, I was good to go, man.

What's odd is, nothing in me changed as a result of these realizations. I just woke up to spiritual truths that had always been there through the years. The things I wanted, I already had hold of – God's unconditional love for me, salvation. My life was safe in His hands. I had all those things, but because of my mental illness, I couldn't enjoy them. As those who struggle with mental illness can tell you, depression is ruthless. It's vicious because it even comes to tear apart your spiritual life. I've often wondered why God allows that. I'm not sure I'll ever know.

I don't know if God wears thin on patience like we humans do. If He does, I sure hope He was plugging his ears as I whined about my salvation. I wonder sometimes, 'What was God thinking during those years of obsessive dorm room bellyaching sessions?' I imagine God nudging Jesus saying, "You better fix this. I can't listen to one more prayer. I've already done it for this dude. I'm going insane. If he asks again, I'm going to take it back. Or maybe I'll send a lightning bolt to end his prayers for good."

Doing Away with Crappy Salvation Theology

I had another major flaw in my theology and it wreaked havoc on my life. It's what I'll call "conditional salvation." It looked a bit like this: Jesus stood in our place and took our punishment for our sin. When we accept this, we're gifted eternal life. This is the gospel message and it's a glorious because we can't earn this gift. When we come to God, we don't have to first make all our wrongs right. The only need is to come as we are and God accepts and forgives that person for free. End of story.

Unfortunately, this message is like a spiritual allergen in the churches I grew up in. Remember the story of dread I've recounted of getting mangled up into a car dashboard? The one where someone dies with sin in their heart? When shitty salvation theology collides with that horror scene, it doesn't bode well for the dying. This is a serious misrepresentation of the biblical message of salvation. Think about it. Someone receives salvation and all is well with the world. But at the time of death they forget to confess a sin resulting in an eternity apart from God. If that's true, Jesus's cross is pretty weak.

Jesus, "God made flesh" rescues us. He loves us so much that He gave himself up. He died with the guilt, shame and responsibility of our sin.

That's a pretty significant exchange that God took on for us. God, the creator of all things, died because He wants us with Him forever. He did what it took to rescue us from our sin, but you mean to tell me, even after dying, it depends on us to maintain our salvation? This is ludicrous.

Imagine you're dirt poor broke and your rich uncle bails you out and pays off your mortgage. He does it out of the goodness of his heart, no strings attached. Once the house is paid off, the house belongs to you. There's nothing else needed for you to maintain ownership of that house. So it would be insane for you to start sending in monthly payments. But this depicts the craziness of "conditional salvation." The reality is that we are given salvation freely and our sin is no longer counted against us.

We will sin more.
It won't be counted against us.
It is finished.
You heard Jesus. Now, shut up and receive the gift!

Before I had a deeper understanding of grace, I treated God like he was an impersonal computer. He required a login and correct password for access to the Heavenly Gates Website. Before I got grace, it was "say the right words" (username). It was "do the right things" (password). It was only after I jumped through those hoops that he would save me and keep me (access to website).

Instead, God loves me. He wants me, and He did what needed to be done to have me. Thankfully, He doesn't let my dumb ass stand in the way of our reconciliation. I still struggle with the concept of grace, and God's unconditional love. But with these new truths in place, I hold firm to a salvation that doesn't waver based on my actions. I've relinquished the need to make sure I'm saved and don't feel impulses to say the "right words." If God hasn't saved me by now, He never will.

The Grace That Saved Me from Drowning

Though I had a healthier perception of God and salvation, I still had dark times of depression. I remember sitting at the end of a pier at Folly Beach in South Carolina. I had frequented this beach as a kid, never once imagining the state of mind that I would bring back with me as an adult. What a contrast. When I was little, I remember playing in the sand with my brother on summer days. Picnicking with the family. On the way home, we'd get a slushy and go to the movies. I was on that same beach. The beach where I'd forged so many fun memories. But this time I wanted to die. I felt like I was at the end of my rope. I had no answers. No hope.

I sat there, head buried between my legs, no care of what I looked like to passersby. I began to beg God to help. I begged Him, knowing that if He wasn't there or didn't help, there was no hope. But, I believe that He began to speak to me.

He told me three things that I'll never forget for the rest of my life. The first was about grace. From that day forward, I would never see grace as only something that saved me from an eternity without God. I'd also see it as a daily need. I believed this in a casual way. But after living a situation out in which I had a severe need for it, it finally sunk into my heart. It was a profound realization.

The verse that reads "my grace is sufficient" (2 Corinthians 12:9) was there for the taking that day at the pier. The question in front of me was whether I believed it was true. At that moment, I decided I had no choice. Either I believed this statement to be true, or I'd crumble and die. I had to hold on to something. At the time of facing so much pain and agonizing desperation, I gave up the hope of being fully rescued. I just needed something to keep me from crumbling completely. This verse had to be true or I was a goner. I decided to actually take what I believe to be Jesus's words as truth.

This belief meant that regardless of the pain, no matter my doubts and lack of light at the end of the tunnel, Jesus is all we need. I didn't feel this truth. It didn't take the pain away. But I had to mentally accept it as true, or there was no hope.

That day on the pier, I reflected on who I was and what I had learned in the past. There were rock solid truths I'd believed all my life. There were people I respected that believed the same way. I decided that I had invested too much into a faith in this savior for me to turn back now. "Yes, I believe."

And, you'll never believe what happened! This dove descended right in front of me. I saw footsteps on the surface of the water, like it was an invisible Jesus walking towards me. It was kind of freaky, but then I felt like I'd snorted a bunch of cocaine. I fell to the ground and I knew everything would be OK because I felt great.

Nope. Just kidding. None of that happened. It was as simple as that. I said, "Lord, I believe what you say." That moment became an anchor in my life. It kept me from spiritual and maybe even physical death. The pain didn't subside, the tears didn't stop falling. I just decided to believe and hoped that in time, God would turn this thing around.

Taking God's Truths with Me Day by Day

But what about tomorrow? Walking away from that pier, the thoughts of the next day scared me to death. I had to lead a staff meeting. I had to counsel people. I had to put on a game-face for my family. I had to talk to people. I had to be a husband, a father, and friend. I had to take responsibility. Sigh. I had to exist, man.

So this is what it means when Jesus says, "Don't worry about tomorrow. Today has enough problems of its own," (Matthew 6:34). And this is the second thing I believe God communicated to me. Well alright then. I don't have the strength to think about tomorrow. The beauty is I don't have to be strong for tomorrow, either. Of course tomorrow will come, but it's not supposed to be a concern for me today. I had enough pain to endure for today. And I'm telling you, this realization of taking one day at a time was a lifesaver.

Knowing I didn't have to worry about tomorrow didn't make me feel completely better. God doesn't promise to give us strength for tomorrow. He tells us not to worry about tomorrow. I'm reminded of the part in the Lord's Prayer that says, "Give us this day our daily bread." I'm not sure if Jesus can make his point any clearer. The meeting tomorrow, the family man stuff tomorrow, the tasks, the getting out of bed, none of that needs to be a concern for me.

This is a life lesson that I'll always have to go back to. And when I don't, that's on me. These instructions of Jesus are a gift to me. I either accept them and use the exact amount of strength that God gave me for today. Or, I try to muscle through today and tomorrow, a feat that God didn't give me enough strength for. Tomorrow, I believe He'll give me enough strength for tomorrow. I'm thankful. It feels as if God has shown me truths to hold onto throughout my life. His grace is enough. His grace is not meant for tomorrow until tomorrow comes. I'm going to die at some point, but it's going to be OK. I've come a long way since those days in the dorm room.

And the third truth is based on James 4:14 when the dude punks out people for being arrogant and boastful about making plans. Have you ever killed a pregnant spider? It's some freaky stuff and I think I've done this twice in my life. I feel extremely privileged. You hit this real fat mom, because you can't just let a spider chill in your house, it could be a black widow or brown recluse, even if it's not brown or black. You never know if it's trying to trick you.

So you hit that spider, killing it but simultaneously birthing a bunch of living spider babies. And then, you obviously can't let a bunch of baby spiders just do their thing. They're baby spiders, but being a baby doesn't count for anything when you have eight legs and grow up to be a mass murderer that catches living animals only to tie up, torture, and eat it later. So, "Hey, little spiders, you are born. Congratulations! Oh, no . . . now, you're dead."

That life was pretty short, but when you think about it, from God's eternal perspective, ours is even shorter. "What is your life? You are a mist that appears for a little while and then vanishes." I don't think Apostle J intended this to be so encouraging, but rather, a sucker punch to the gut for anyone that needed some perspective. For this morbid homeboy, knowing from God's perspective, a perspective that is foreign to me, my life is as short as baby birthed spider gone dead right away warms my heart. I have this hope that one day, my perspective of time will change and be more conformed to God's. At that time, I'll also see my pain and suffering on His level. For some reason, this is like ice cold Kool-Aid aide on a hot summer day.

The Gospel Passage That Never Stuck

Remember back to the opening chapter on the day that my mind got blown by a passage in Romans 4? If not, here's a reminder. I was going through my "daily devotions" reading the Bible and praying, when I came across Romans 4:4-8.

> *Now to the one who works, his wages are not counted as a gift but as his due. And to the one who does not work but believes in him who justifies the ungodly, his faith is counted as righteousness, just as David also speaks of the blessing of the one to whom God counts righteousness apart from works:*

> *"Blessed are those whose lawless deeds are forgiven, and whose sins are covered; blessed is the man against whom the Lord will not count his sin."*

I came out of my room in amazement asking my dad if this verse was true. My dad confirmed it. And yet, in all my years of church-going, this was not the free message of grace that I heard. My OCD brain didn't help either. Surely I had to get my ass in gear and be a "good Christian." Salvation couldn't be that free. But it was.

Now all of these years later, I have a different take on the idea of "accepting Jesus," "getting saved," and "becoming born-again." That Romans 4 revelation all those years ago was the moment I caught a glimpse of gospel truth. And now I've had years to reflect on whether or not that moment was my moment of "salvation," so to speak—the moment I got "saved." Little did I know at the time that the question of my salvation would plague me with immense stress, pain, and sadness. I lived a life of rituals, constant fear, and total lack of spiritual security.

In the church circles, I grew up with a great deal of emphasis on saying the Sinner's Prayer, as if once we accept Jesus, our prayers are no longer coming from a sinner. But the thing is, we still do bad stuff that make us sinners that are declared righteous. I know families to this day that believe if they could just get their kid to "say the prayer," they'd have salvation, as if it's a result of a verbal formula. There is so much emphasis placed on this moment of saying the prayer that many Christians hold to the belief that if you don't remember when you accepted Christ (i.e., said the Sinner's Prayer), you can't be really saved. I've actually been the recipient of that allegation, accused of being a "non-Christian" because of my inability to recount that special moment of transformation. Although I do believe in a transformation, I do not believe it's always discernible or results in "sweat and tears." As a former pastor of mine used to declare, "No tears, not real." What a weenie theology.

I no longer view salvation this way. I've talked to people before who were seeking God and had not said "the magical prayer," but who were compelled to keep coming to Jesus asking for food, believing or hoping that's where it's to be found—without the faith to simply partake without reservation. I've been convinced in some of these instances that many of these folks are just as secure as the old-school Christian of thirty years. The Holy Spirit is revealing truth to them, leading them to God's love, but they don't quite have the mental assent to put it altogether with clarity. I could be dead wrong.

Nowadays, when people ask me when I was "saved," instead of getting a panic attack, digging out my salvation checklist and getting crippled by worry and doubt, I simply say that I don't know when I received God's love. I don't believe God works through formulas, and I discard the notion that I can even have it all figured out. I just believe that I'm secure in the hands of a God that loves me. I believe what He says over what my OCD and depression tells me. #HowYouLikeMeNow

POSTFACE

—

Hello, reader. Joey here, the crazy guy you just read about. I want to present you with a great opportunity. Please use my personal stories of utter pain and anguish to talk amongst yourselves about your own junk. That may sound overly simplistic, I know. Unfortunately, "talking" is far from simplistic in American culture, and specifically in church culture.

Before I talk more about talking, I wrote this book for a myriad of reasons. I've tried to give the mentally ill some helpful advice. I've also tried to offer advice to those who interact regularly with mentally ill loved ones. I've done the best that I can through counseling, taking medication, and going on with life. But despite being plagued with depression and OCD, I hope I was of help to you. Believe it or not, through past experiences, yours truly has counseled others. I've found that being transparent about my personal mental illness sets something free in other people's minds. I can't count the number of hesitant people who fear being candid about their mental illness. That is, until I opened up. And then? Open the emotional floodgates. Because if a dude people call "pastor" is as sick as I am—and I can talk about it—then they're that much freer to share their own struggles.

I believe sharing my experiences and giving advice has value. But my biggest hope is that this book will act as a catalyst to start conversations. I'm sure some of you are saying things like, "OMG, can you believe Joey showed the old man his penis?!" Go ahead, have your laughs. No, what I'm talking about is deeper and more significant. There are some major obstacles in the way of transparent conversation.

You don't believe me? Well, let me ask you this: Why is a book like this unique? Because I'm a pastor. Whether you or I like it or not, people look to me for leadership. They look at me to take cues. Unfortunately, many people in my shoes lead by the poorest example imaginable. Leaders talk so much about the significance of leading well, but they rarely, if ever, talk with complete candor, openness, or honesty about their past and present struggles. I'll let you in on a little secret. I'm not the only messed up leader in the church. There's a lot of other mentally ill pastors. There are many leaders in the church addicted to pornography, alcohol, or overeating. There are many "role models" consumed with building a huge social media platform and gave up on the pursuit of humility years ago. We have a big problem on our hands. There's a younger generation out there who have highly sensitive BS detectors. They're usually tech-savvy, DIYers, grassroots-focused, organic-eating, people-centered, cause-driven, fake-shunning millennials. And they're moving on from inauthentic relationships and institutions. They don't trust people who avoid having their weaknesses exposed. Unfortunately, many churches represent the most negative examples.

In response, us church people do the worst thing possible. We present ourselves as having stuff figured out. We want to present ourselves as those who have theological and moral answers for the hurting. But this attitude completely counters the central message of for whom the church exists. We are all broken people in need. We are not answer suppliers.

When leaders keep their struggles secret to maintain credibility, they set others up to fail. And if I've heard it once, I've heard it a thousand times: "I have a smaller group of people that I'm open with."

Well, thanks for being so open with a few people, Mr. or Ms. Leader, as you present yourself as a hero to the masses. For your information, your followers are busting tail, aspiring to something you don't live out yourself. By the way, we just found out that you weren't even listening to the small group of folks you surround yourself with.

At some point soon, the predicament of hiding behind a mask will be long gone, because everyone is going to stop trusting you. Your need to self-protect and convince others of being worthy of following.

OK, I'll get off my soap box now. Here's my point: Those who value authenticity and truth-telling, just know that you can't demand this attitude from others, especially when people feel a need to build mutual trust within a discussion group. Before you start using these group questions, talk about what you want to get out of the group. Talk about what feels safe in sharing and what doesn't. Use the questions below as you see fit. They're just suggestions after all. The point is, let's talk about things that are hard and awkward. Because talking it out helps.

If you remember reading the intro to this book, I wholeheartedly believe authenticity is important, not only for my own mental health, but for others who struggle. I got specific about my struggles and sins in the hopes that my authenticity will help others not feel so alone. Now, are you willing to be specific about your struggles with others? See the examples below:

THIS → "I'm beginning to realize I rarely think I'm wrong, and I end up belittling my wife when we argue. I feel like crap about it, but feel so defensive. I don't know what to do."

NOT THIS → "I struggle with pride."

1. Do you feel unsafe being open, honest and transparent about your life? Why?
2. In the gospels, Jesus welcomes hurting broken people. Is there any bit of brokenness you don't think he'd be willing to accept?

Chapter One

1. It's obvious that Joey's issues were a combination of mental illness and the religious church culture he was raised in. Can you relate to having to unlearn unhelpful beliefs that were instilled in you at an early age? What are those things?

2. Let's talk about the Bible for a second. At a young age, Joey had a huge revelation reading about free salvation in Romans 4. Have you had too-good-to-be-true moments like that?

3. Joey has had some extreme repeat behaviors. Sometimes these behaviors could be intensified due to high pressure church environments or beliefs. Have you ever felt compelled to do certain rituals out of duty or fear?

4. Joey has tended to minimize his struggles. Are there things in your own life that you're tempted to sweep under the rug, or say "it's not a big deal" when maybe it is? (Tip: the "struggle" doesn't have to be an issue of mental illness.)

Chapter Two

1. When you read this chapter, did you relate to any wrongheaded beliefs in your past (or present) that have kept you from really seeing God for who He is?

2. Have you ever done things you'd rather not do out of a sense of "religious duty"?

3. Joey thought he was being a "bold witness" for Christ when he gave his speech about Heidel's suicide. Do you have a cringe-worthy
story like that to tell? What would you do different today?

Chapter Three

1. Based on observation or experience with yourself or your kids, what are your general feelings about youth ministry?
2. How can youth be encouraged to shun evil without being afraid of it?

Chapter Four

1. Have you ever made a mistake that you hid out of fear of being seen as a "bad Christian"?
2. For those of you that are Bible readers, how would you describe Joey's misunderstanding of grace?

Chapter Five

1. Have you ever felt responsible to correct someone's beliefs?
2. Have you ever broken off a friendship because your friend believed differently than you?
3. If you regret breaking off a friendship because of differing beliefs, what would you do differently today?
4. Is there anyone in your life you've been judgmental with whom you could make amends?

Chapter Six

1. Have you ever been convinced that God told you something that He didn't actually tell you?
2. Is it possible to hear clearly from God? How can you know?
3. Can you recall times in your life when you felt anxiety over your relationship with God? Were there any rituals you felt like you had to perform in order to be "good with God" again?

Chapter Seven

1. Did your parents talk to you openly about sex when you were a kid? Were you comfortable asking questions about things you didn't understand?
2. Can you recall anything funny you falsely believed about your sexuality?
3. Have you ever had awkward moments of sex-related conversation with your parents or a pastor?
4. Do you feel like you have friends you can talk to openly about issues related to sex?

Chapter Eight

1. What is your most challenging personality flaw, according to your spouse?
2. Was he/she aware of those challenges before committing themselves in marriage?
3. Married folks, do you have a funny or awkward story to tell about a botched proposal?
4. Do you have guilt, shame, or regret over something funny, awkward, or stupid you've done in a relationship, past or present?

Chapter Nine

1. Can you recall when you've been sorely disappointed in something not living up to your expectation?
2. Most churches teach strict abstinence-only sex codes. If you grew up or currently attend a church like this, have you ever felt shamed by that message?

3. Has your church helped you process sexual mistakes? Has your church helped prepare you for how to think about sex in marriage?
4. Do you agree or disagree with Joey's analysis on how the church perceives sex and what relevance premarital sex can have on the longevity of one's marriage?
5. Have you ever been selfish about sex with your spouse?
6. Married folks, do you have a story about a bummer honeymoon?

Chapter Ten

1. Sometimes, answers to life's tough questions and struggles come slowly. Sometimes, it seems like they don't ever come. In Joey's case, finding some help for his depression was a long process. Have you ever struggled with having to wait for an answer when times were hard?
2. Have you ever struggled with depression? Can you explain what it feels like? Have you experienced any help or relief?
3. There's more and more awareness and understanding about depression. But there's still a stigma attached to mental illness. Why do you think that is?

Chapter Eleven

1. Do you have a loved one who has had challenges with mental illness? What has that been like for you?
2. Has this book challenged your understanding or attitude about mental illness? How?
3. Those of you who struggle with mental illness, have you gotten help from a counselor or psychiatrist?
4. Why is it so important for the mentally ill to be open,

honest, and transparent about their struggle?

5. Have you ever told a struggling depressed person a Christian "bumper sticker" answer to their problem?

6. After reading Joey's list of 14 advice tips, which ones resonate with you the most?

Chapter Twelve

1. What do you think the true purpose of prayer is?

2. We're told that religion is supposed to bring us freedom and joy. Sadly, the message we hear in our churches often brings bondage and heartache. What has your experience been like in the church?

3. In your day-to-day life, do you think God is against you? Why?

4. Reflect on this a bit: Joey's mental illness kept him handicapped in such a way that he could not accept or embrace comforting spiritual truths. Have you ever felt unable to accept comforting spiritual truths?

5. Recall the story of Joey at the beach when he was at the end of his rope. Do you have an end-of-your-rope story?

6. Jesus said to "not worry about tomorrow." What are you currently worrying about?

24/7 LIVECHAT
NOW AVAILABLE
IT'S OKAY TO NOT BE OKAY
ANTHEMOFHOPE.ORG
A NON-PROFIT ORGANIZATION
EDICATED TO ILLUMINATING HOPE FOR THOSE
ATTLING BROKENNESS, DEPRESSION, ANXIETY,
SELF-HARM, SUICIDE AND ADDICTION.
@ANTHEMOFHOPE

Made in the USA
San Bernardino, CA
29 November 2017